Peter Spin[illegible] [illegible]007

C000246398

Up The Valley

'memoirs of nowt but a bairn'

by

Lorna Laidler

Published by Lorwil Publishing 2003
18 Crumstone Court
Killingworth
Newcastle upon Tyne
NE12 6SZ

Copyright © Lorna Laidler

All right reserved. No part of this publication may be reproduced or transmitted in any form without the express permission, in writing of the publisher.

ISBN 0-9546475-0-5

1st Reprint 2004
2nd Reprint 2006

Printed in Great Britain by L & S Printers,
Camperdown, Tyne & Wear
Tel: 0191 2161717

Also published by Lorwil Publishing

Down The Town

by

Lorna Laidler

ISBN 0-9546475-2-1

Granda and Nana Nairn

For my Grandchildren

This book is a work of faction, a mixture of family stories and my childhood memories. Some of the family stories actually took place in other parts of Northumberland, but for the sake of simplicity I have set them all 'Up the Valley'. I apologise if my memory of some events is at variance with the memories of others, but I was 'nowt but a bairn'. A few names have been changed to protect the innocent.
Lorna E. Laidler

Index

Poems

Drawings

Drawings (cont)

Photographs

Chapter One – Windyhaugh

The family car meandered up the valley between the green domed Cheviot Hills, with their occasional circular stone sheep stells. The road followed the path of the river Coquet; little more than a mountain stream this high up the valley. It passed the sheep pens and the tiny incongruous dance hall, donated to this isolated and scattered community by some long dead benefactor. My heart lifted as Barrowburn farm came into sight, nestling at the foot of the hills in the early summer sunshine.

If Liza had still been there, no doubt she'd have been out in the yard feeding the hens, or doing some other little job which would bring her outdoors long enough to give the passing car a good look over.

Dear Liza, passing cars were a rarity in her day, and she did like to know where they were going and what business their occupants had in this forgotten corner. Not that she would admit to being the valley's lookout mind you, oh no! But now and then she gave herself away. Like the time she said to my Granda in tones of innocent inquiry, "I heared a green van gan up the valley the other day Jack?" and waited, her pinny full of hen meal, until her curiosity had been satisfied.

Homesteads hereabouts are built in twos, within a good shout of each other, then miles of hills and sheep, before the next two. Barrowburn was Windyhaugh's neighbour. The two grey stone houses with their attendant byre stables and haysheds were about quarter of a mile apart, huddled together for company in the empty landscape.

I glanced at my three city born sons in the back of the car. Their neutral faces told me that this place meant nothing to them. It was foolish to think that it would-they had no ties here no memories.

Memories! Here we were at Windyhaugh. My husband, knowing me well, pulled over onto the wide grass verge and we looked over the river at the sturdy stone house set in a widening of the valley floor, the haugh that gave the farm its name. The wooden footbridge across the Coquet was still there, so were the two ash trees near the foot of the hill, beneath which John Wesley was reputed to have preached and which was my launching pad when I played roly-poly. At the end of the bridge someone had planted a square of conifers, new since my time and I felt a surge of resentment that anyone should tamper with Windyhaugh. Ridiculous really, I'd never even lived there and had no claim on the place. The conifer planters probably owned it now and so had every right to plant them or anything else, which took their fancy. I looked beyond the offending trees.

The old place was looking very neat and tidy, a narrow strip of garden edged the front of the house with bright summer blooms and I smiled at the memory of Nana struggling to protect her strip of lupins and marigolds with chicken wire from the marauding hens.

The house was set looking up and down the valley, so from the road I had a side on view. The farmyard behind the house was immaculate as was the row of outbuildings and the hayshed looming behind them. I had no doubt that the small walled garden, which I knew lay beyond would be similarly neat. The present occupants are to be commended I thought. The place looked efficient. I wondered why this should depress me. What was missing?

"Why have we stopped here Dad?" Called a voice from the back of the car. "My grandparents and two uncles used to live here, and I spent quite a lot of my childhood on this farm" I answered ignoring the pitying looks "Would you like to walk along by the river? You might see a trout" We climbed out and the boys hared off down the river with their dad behind them, while I sat down on the grass, gazed over at Windyhaugh, and remembered what it was that was missing.

Nana always had hens scratching round the place, and ducks platching about by the river. Granda's Border terrier, Teaser and the three border collies, Tip, Bett, and Sheddles were always there or thereabouts. Sally, the massive black and white pig grunted from the sty beside the garden gate, and Dick, the carthorse lived in the field half way up the hill behind the house. Dante' the tortoiseshell cat hid her kittens about the farm, and the two house cows, Daisy and Dolly steadily grazed their way round the field behind the hayshed.

That's why the place looked so tidy.... and empty, no animals except a few sheep dotted about the hills. No doubt people bought their bacon and eggs at the shop and everything would be mechanised now. They'd even have refinements like a telephone and electricity, unheard of in Nana and Granda's day. Perhaps they even rounded up the sheep on quad bikes, although I couldn't imagine anything except a sheepdog negotiating some of the steeper slopes. If children lived here now, they certainly weren't out playing in the stackyard the way my cousin; Alan and I would have been— probably sitting inside watching T.V. Like any town child, I thought. We were hardly in the house at all, except to eat and sleep. Oh yes, and on one occasion when Nana locked me in because a load of lime had been delivered to sweeten the hill land, and she was terrified I'd get burned by it. I was scared of lime for years afterwards, imagining it to be as great a danger as sulphuric acid, or nuclear fall out! I smiled; remembering Nana wringing her hands anxiously until the lime was safely distributed to the far reaches of the farm. Happy days!

I lay back on the sheep-cropped grass and closed my eyes, letting my ears take over. The river gurgled in the background, as I thought back to the time on this hill farm when I was five years old, summers were warm and fragrant with the smell of hay, Nana made rabbit pies for dinner, uncle Bill made me laugh and Granda called me "The little maid".

The Author in 1949

Chapter Two- Barrowburn

I was a lucky child, living most of the year with my parents, and later, my little sister, Linda, in a row of terraced houses running down to the river Tyne, but spending my summers with Nana, Granda and uncles Bill and Jim at Windyhaugh. Getting me there was quite an expedition. No one had cars then, at least no one we knew, and so Mam and I got the red United bus in Newcastle and headed north to Morpeth to catch the Rothbury bus. Once a week, on a Saturday, it made two journeys up the Coquet valley past Rothbury, passing even the tiny village of Alwinton and stopping at the Windyhaugh dance hall, right next to Barrowburn and within half a mile of our final destination. Travelling by Wells Fargo in the Wild West must have been something like that journey. The bus, which delivered parcels and all manner of goods, as well as people, clattered and wheezed it's way out of the city and into the rolling green Northumbrian countryside, which became wilder and emptier as we approached the pretty market town of Rothbury on the edge of the Cheviots. Here most of the passengers would disembark, usually leaving only us hardy souls to press on right into the hills.

I used to imagine that Mam and I were explorers, or on a wagon train in the Wild West. I felt sorry for the poor folk who could only go as far as Rothbury and were unaware of the delights of upper Coquetdale a few miles further on, but a world away.
Occasionally, there would be someone going as far as Alwinton. A shepherd maybe, who'd ventured into Rothbury to buy a new pair of tackety boots with turned up toes, handmade by Rogerson's of Rothbury, like the ones Granda and my uncles always wore. But in all the times we went on that bus there was never anyone else going as far as Windyhaugh, which reinforced my belief that the valley was a secret world, known only to it's sparse inhabitants and a few privileged souls like me.

We even had to run the gauntlet of an army checkpoint. A soldier in a little sentry box manned a barrier across the road, just past Alwinton, which he obligingly raised once he had given you the once over. We would step off the bus at the dance hall and wave to the driver as he turned for the return journey to civilisation. Then, off we would go, with a spring in our step to our first port of call, through the big farm gate to Barrowburn, the hub of upper Coquetdale and home of Liza and Geordie Murray and their daughter, Mary.

Geordie Murray and flock heading back to Barrowburn

Hospitality at Barrowburn was legendary. There was even an article about it once in the Newcastle Journal, fame indeed for country folk. Passing through the picturesque farmyard with the burn running through it, we were invariably greeted by the sight of Mary's rear end

<u>Mary of Barrowburn</u>

as she scrubbed the stone flagged entrance passage on her hands and knees. (Barrowburn's front passage must have been the cleanest in the county, Mary scrubbed it so often.) She would leap up and greet us kindly with a "Come away in, you must be fair famished" as though we'd travelled from the other end of the country, not the county.

Liza herself, foursquare in her wrap around pinny, would welcome us into the house, eyes twinkling behind her glasses, and seat us on a form by the table on which tea and scones would be set with a triumphant flourish. Liza's aged mother, Mrs Barton would be seated regally by the fire, looking like old Queen Mary Indeed, she was a very important person hereabouts, having served as the community's midwife for most of her life.

She would travel to the widely dispersed hill farms on a pony in all weathers to deliver new generations.

Such activity seemed hard to believe of her now, presiding over the household from her straight-backed chair beside the most fascinating fireplace I have ever seen.

It was a black leaded range, polished assiduously to gleaming magnificence by Liza every morning. The fire itself was flanked on one side by an oven and on the other by a set-pot full of water, kept permanently hot by the peat fire. Swinging overhead, like a metal gallows was the "yettling-on-a-swee" - a device for suspending the huge black cauldron, in which Liza always had a stew bubbling or blackcurrant jam in the making. Swivelling across the fire from each side were two metal plates on which rested the blackened kettle and a pan and separating the whole thing from the rest of the room was a gleaming brass fender. The rest of the room was equally remarkable. The low ceiling, slung with beams, resembled nothing so much as a massive magazine rack, its credentials as a fire hazard were second to none, as stuffed between beams and ceiling, were huge quantities of "Farmer's Weeklies" and bundles of hazel shanks waiting to be turned into dressed sticks - the beautifully carved horn headed walking sticks used by everyone in the hills. Suspended from the beams were well-patronised strips of sticky brown flypaper and, as at Windyhaugh, hanging between them, were sides of home cured bacon, (no qualms about EU hygiene rules then).

The floor was a stone flagged and covered by colourful clippie mat, made from strips cut from old clothes. The wooden mat frame with the hessian base stretched across it leaned against one wall. The deep windowsill set in the thickness of the outer wall was crowded with pots of bright geraniums, in my memory, always in bloom.

In the far corner squatted a huge brass bedstead with a feather mattress covered by a multicoloured patchwork quilt, and staring glassily down on it from the wall above, was a fox's head mounted on a wooden plaque. Geordie used to tell me that if I went outside, I would see the fox's rear end protruding from the outer wall, but I never could find it. In the middle of the room stood a large well-scrubbed table, surrounded by wooden forms.

On one occasion, Jen Brodie, younger daughter of the Blindburn household, further up the valley called in to find the whole family about to eat their dinner - Mrs Barton, Liza, Geordie, Mary and "Old Tom of Barrowburn", a man of many years and few words, who had worked there as the hired hand since he was a boy. They made space for Jen around the table with rumbles of welcome and kind inquiries.

"Wad ee like some hashy?" asked Liza, in her singsong Northumbrian tones. They wad, so it was dolloped onto their plates, steaming mounds of mutton stew. Everyone, except Jen, polished theirs off quickly. Back came Liza with a large bowl of tinned fruit.

"Wad ee like some peaches?".

They wad, so they were spooned onto the same plates, already polished clean with chunks of bread - all except Jen's. Her peaches were dumped unceremoniously on top of the remaining "hashy" I still don't know whether she managed to eat them or not!

Having renewed old friendships at Barrowburn, we set off on the short walk up the track to Windyhaugh.

<u>Mam and Linda on the footbridge to Windyhaugh</u>

I ran ahead as the wooden footbridge came into view and clattered over it, excitement mounting, as I saw the tall dark haired figure of uncle Bill in the front field - a hayfield this year. Other years it would grow turnips, potatoes, barley or oats. With his long strides, uncle Bill came to meet me and grinning broadly swept me up whirling me through the air onto his shoulders.

"Hallow there Lorna Doon and up again". This was a little joke about my name of which he never tired. Turning to greet my mother, he took my case from her and the three of us ambled through the hay towards the house. I sighed with contentment at the prospect of another carefree summer.

Chapter Three - Fire, Cows and Cats.

"Is the little maid up yet?" Called Granda, clumping in from looking the sheep, shepherd's crook in one hand and rabbit hanging lifeless from the other. I ran to him for a cuddle and a dry shave, his and Bill's usual morning greeting, which was to rub my cheeks rosy with their unshaven bristles. The rabbit was dumped unceremoniously on the kitchen table and Nana swept it up to be carried into the scullery and transformed into rabbit pie. Granda put me down on the clippie mat in front of the unlit fire and hauled handfuls of field mushrooms from his jacket pocket.

"There y'are maidie, that'll make a grand breakfast with a bit bacon". His brown eyes twinkled at me as he flopped down into the fireside chair. Nana's considerable bulk lumbered back into the kitchen.

"I better light yon fire", she mumbled, more to herself than anyone else. Nana often talked to herself, a symptom of her lonely life-style. Mam had gone back to Newcastle on the previous evening's bus, so she'd had adult female company for only half a day.

The lighting of the fire never ceased to excite me. It was meticulously laid with rolled up Newcastle Journals and Farmers Weeklies, kindling sticks, and either peat or sea coal, depending on the state of finances at the time. Nana would approach the huge black leaded fireplace, confidently bearing a big enamel jug of paraffin and a match. She would strike the match against the hearth and light the edge of a Farmer's Weekly, which would curl and turn feebly brown. Then she would take a step back, grasp the jug firmly and hurl a dose of paraffin onto the fire. The resulting conflagration was nothing short of spectacular. The fire would explode up the chimney, roaring like a train in a tunnel.

"Ye'll set haad ti the hoos yin 'o' these days", Granda would mutter.

Sometimes she overdid the paraffin and the fire looked like taking over the whole chimney. When this happened, salt was sprinkled on to tame it. On the other hand, on the rare occasions when the fire's roar died to whimper and looked like failing, a handful of sugar was used to revive it - simple household remedies we have forgotten in this centrally heated age.

Once the fire was "away", the frying pan was set on it and slabs of thick, salty bacon, cut from one of the sides hanging from the ceiling, were cooked until crispy. I had already stalked and peeled the mushrooms, a very responsible job for a five-year-old. Each one had to be examined meticulously for the tell tale holes which gave away maggots in residence. They looked like woodworm holes in old furniture and any mushrooms displaying them were consigned to the flames.

Breakfast over, Granda took the galvanised metal bucket from the scullery and with me shadowing him, strode across the yard to the byre opposite the back door, scattering hens with every step.

The byre was gloomy and smelled richly of manure and poultry, as the hen house, a sort of wooden cage, was suspended over one corner. It had a narrow wooden ramp, like a miniature ship's gangplank, leading up to it to afford access to hens and people. There was a door leading through to the hayshed opposite the one by which we had entered. On the left was a square area full of the paraphernalia needed on the farm, string, wire, nails, tins of sheep dip and the like. There was also a fearsome machine looking like a monstrous cross between a mangle and a cement mixer. This was for chopping up turnips for the sheep's winter-feed. The two cow stalls were on the right, but only one was occupied. Dolly, the shorthorn cow, turned and stared balefully at Granda, as he placed the bucket beneath her udder and the milking stool beneath his buttocks with one fluid movement. Then, leaning his head against her flanks, his cap on skew wiff, he coaxed the milk from her, splashing it into the bucket, noisily at first, then with a quiet hissing noise as the bucket filled.

At this point, Dante invariably appeared. She was a very pretty cat, white and tortoiseshell, a good mouser, a good breeder of kittens and infinitely patient with me. Many's the time she submitted to being pushed round the farmyard in my home made doll's pram, dressed in my doll's clothes, bonnet and all. She looked like a scaled down version of the wolf in Red Riding Hood. But at milking time she was all cat, ingratiating herself with Granda by rubbing round his ankles and purring loudly, frantic to please him in case he forgot to fill her saucer with Dolly's warm milk. He always did remember, of course, and if Dante had kittens of an age to lap, they would creep from dark corners to join her at the saucer. If I kept very still, they wouldn't scatter, so I always held my breath and crouched small, in the hopes of seeing these beautiful, shy creatures. Sometimes I was privileged to touch them, before they melted back into the hayshed or wherever else they hid.

Dante and I were co-conspirators in hiding her kittens. She and I knew that if Granda found them before their eyes were open, he would "make sailors of them" in the rain barrel, but if we kept them concealed until they could look him in the eye, he hadn't the heart to harm them.

Hearth and Home

Nana lit the fire with a flourish every day
The paraffin she threw on ensured it was in to stay
The flames roared up the chimney before they settled down
"Howt lass! Ye'll set the hoose ahad," said Granda with a frown

The fire warmed the household; it cooked our daily bread,
It burned up all the rubbish and it kept the family fed
The sickly lambs revived by it, evenings sped by in its gleam
The tin bath set in front of it was how we all kept clean.

The fire would burn less brightly as the day drew to a close
With mugs of cocoa, round the hearth we'd sit and warm our toes
The ashes overnight would cool and fall into the tray
Next morning they were cleared and raked to start another day.

Chapter Four - Granda's Garden.

"Haway lassie! Are ye ganna feed thor hens or no?" Nana's voice called from the scullery door. I jumped and the kittens scattered, "I'm coming Nana." Much as I loved Dante and the kittens, I couldn't neglect my considerable responsibilities. As I ran in the back door, Nana was lifting the lid from a large plywood bin in the corner of the scullery and filling a battered enamel dish with corn for the hens. They, impatient for their feed were already in the scullery, clucking and tutting.

"Hout! Git oot!" Exclaimed Nana, flapping ineffectually at the tide of Rhode Island Reds. They circumnavigated her easily, and only vacated the scullery when I, like the Pied Piper, led them out into the yard, flinging handfuls of corn far and wide.

Feeding 'thor hens'

The normally slow creatures would run hither and thither, in a frenzy to eat the corn before their sisters. All of this activity was beneath Jock, the cockerel. He strode majestically among them, the sun glinting blue and green in his magnificent tail feathers, pecking disdainfully at the corn and looking down his beak at us all.

This task completed, I was free to do as I pleased. I wandered over to the pigsty Sally, the huge saddleback sow, grunted and snuffled as I leaned over the stone wall to scratch her bristly back. She and I were old friends. She would even let me ride her round the farmyard on the rare occasions when she was freed from the confines of her sty. This wasn't very often though, so I made a point of visiting her to relieve what I imagined must be a life of unremitting boredom. She especially liked it when I took the besom, as I had this morning. It was rather unwieldy in my small hands, but I heaved it over the wall and scrubbed her back. Sally grunted blissfully and flopped down on her side with a soporific smile on her face. If pigs could purr, she would.

This was very satisfying for both of us. I was glad to make Sally happy, and she more than repaid me by her obvious pleasure. The only drawback to visiting Sally was the smell. Even with a regular clean out, she still tended to wiff a bit, so after a while, I propped the besom against the wall and wandered through the gate into the garden.

Looking back, I don't know how Granda found the time to make his garden into the paradise it was. Like "The Secret Garden ", it was hidden by a wall, but it had a pigsty on one side, a dry toilet on the other, and a Cheviot hill at it's back. It was set in a windswept valley in north Northumberland, and yet, it bloomed as though it was in more cosseted southern climes.
I heard the gate click behind me and Granda's curly toed boots crunch on the gravel path.

"Now then little maid", he greeted me. "Are you looking at the cheeky faces?"

They, in the world outside Granda's garden, were called pansies. These ones had faces the size of saucers, and looked up at me from the edge of the path with impish smiles. I took Granda's hand and we wandered quietly among his flowers. Dahlias were his speciality, gorgeous, flamboyant coloured blooms, but the snapdragons were bonny too, and I loved to pick the odd one and make its mouth open and close with a squeeze of my fingers.

Granda lifted the graipe and began manuring his beloved flowers. I stopped by the southernwood and crushed a piece between my fingers to savour its heady scent. Then I wandered on to gaze at the plant I admired most in the whole garden. It was a towering thistle, the ornamental kind I have since seen in the gardens of Hollyrood Palace. It wasn't so much a pretty plant, but very handsome, with its silver green foliage and purple flower. I loved it, but was terrified that Granda would notice it.

For if he did, and surely he couldn't fail to (it was as tall as him and his sons, at over six foot) he would be bound to lash it down with his shepherd's stick, the way he lashed angrily at the thistles on the hill outside.

"Crunch", went the gravel, and Granda was beside me looking at the thistle. My heart leaped into my throat, surely, he would cut it down now, and he was looking straight at it. Instead, he looked from the plant to me "Aye, it's a grand flower right enough. Yon's a scotch thistle from ower the border", he said, and walked away out of the garden.

Relief flooded through me at the reprieve, but it was a long time before I understood why Granda waged a battle against the thistles on the farm, and nurtured this one in his garden.

Granda's garden

Chapter Five - The Corral.

I strolled back to the house for a drink of milk. Dolly's milk was delicious, with an earthy flavour boiled out of the sanitised stuff we drink today. Nana was busy in the stone flagged walk-in pantry, ("The Milkus" or milk house). She was messing about with the milk, and a Heath Robinson looking contraption called the separator, consisting of a lot of metal pans and spouts piled precariously on top of each other. Its workings were a mystery to me, but the end result was rich cream separated from rest of the milk.

"Wad ee like a torn at the chorn?" Asked Nana. The churn was a wooden cask on a stand with a handle at one end. Once the cream was put in, Nana would turn the handle and in no time, it seemed, we had home made butter, mouth watering, and pale yellow stuff.

I took the handle and turned it. It was surprisingly heavy and the novelty soon wore off this monotonous occupation. Nana smilingly took over and I ran out to see what was doing around the farm.

Uncles Bill and Jim were mending dry stone walls somewhere out on the hill, so I couldn't pester them. I'd heard Granda drive the little grey Ferguson tractor out of the stackyard a moment or two before, so he was out of range too. I would have to amuse myself.

I ambled through the stackyard behind the hayshed. Leaning on the sun-warmed wall, (there weren't many fences in the hills, stone walls were what divided field from hill) I contemplated Dolly and her younger companion, Daisy, (also a shorthorn). Casting my mind back to the western I had seen recently at our neighbourhood fleapit, I pictured the cowboys riding the range and leaping corral fences on their magnificent steeds.

I looked around. The lack of fences to jump was a bit of a problem, but wait! We did have a sort of corral - the sheep pens! They would do and Dolly could be my steed.

I opened the field gate and headed for Dolly, who was stolidly chewing the cud. Cows are very nosy creatures, and she clearly wondered at this departure from her routine. After all, she had been milked this morning, and the next landmark in her day would normally be the evening milking. Her head lifted and she wandered over to meet me, followed by Daisy. I reached for her right horn, and after an initial toss of her head, she allowed me to lead her out of the field and into the sheep pens, and of course, Daisy came too.

I closed the gate, corralling the pair of them, and then hanging onto Dolly's horn with one hand; I grasped the top bar of the gate with the other and climbed up. It was difficult keeping Dolly close enough to the gate for me to step from one to the other, but eventually, I managed it and was astride her bony back, hanging onto her horns like handlebars.

Dolly was a bitter disappointment. She didn't react a bit like the horses in cowboy films. She tossed her head, rolled her eyes, and with a mournful "Moo", set off in a sort of sideways dance around the sheep pen, with me clinging precariously to her. Daisy had evidently never seen the like! And the sight of her normally placid companion behaving in such a way filled her with alarm. With a high-pitched wail more like a donkey's bray than a moo, she attempted to make her escape. Unfortunately, the only exit open to her was the one leading to the dipping bath, the sunken trough, where sheep were periodically dipped in foul smelling yellow disinfectant. Thankfully, it was empty, because Daisy ran straight down the ramp, which the sheep normally scrambled up, on their way out.

The side facing her had no such aid to escape it was a straight edge over which the sheep were dropped, struggling, into the dip. The trough was narrow, no wider than Daisy herself, and, since she was not inclined to walk backwards up the ramp, she was stuck there, bellowing her distress to the sky.

I slid down off Dolly, grabbed the tasselled end of Daisy's tail, and pulled hard. She didn't budge an inch, but her bellowing increased to such a pitch, that it brought Nana out of the house.
"Hout! What hev ee was up to noo lassie? What's Dolly dee'n in the sheep pens? Howay now, take her back ti the field like a good lass."

She turned to go back into the house, but in mid turn, her eye lit on Daisy's face gazing imploringly at her over the edge of the trough.
"Marcy me! The coo's in the sheep dip! Noo what'll we dee?" Then "Jack! Bill! Jim! Where the hell are yee all? The bairn's dippin' the coo!"
"I didn't mean it Nana," I said, beginning to worry about the consequences of my little game. Nana was clearly very agitated, alternately wringing her hands and muttering " Noo what'll we dee?"

Perhaps Granda and my uncles would be angry. They all had fiery tempers, though quick to die down. I felt hot tears spring to my eyes and my lip began to tremble "There there noo lassie, dinna greet". Nana folded me to her ample bosom and cuddled me in. "Your Granda'll fettle it, dinna greet."

"How! What's gannin on doon theyor?"

I heard uncle Bill's voice from the hill above me. I lifted my head to see him striding down towards us, with his long legged shepherd's lope, Tip and Bett at his heels. In moments, uncle Bill was at the sheep a pen.

He leaned on the fence and to my surprise, threw back his dark head and roared with laughter.
"Well I'll be damned! That's the funniest thing I've seen since the watter bailiff fell in the burn!" He howled with mirth, tears streaming down his face. I began to cheer up. Uncle Bill liked a good laugh and I had obviously supplied him with one. I struggled down from Nana' s embrace and tried to explain to him about cowboys and horses and corrals in the Wild West.

This only made him laugh all the more, and it was some time before he was calm enough to say, "Howay then Hopalong Cassidy, we'd best get these lil ol' dogies back on the range " He opened the sheep pen gate and with a whistle or two, Tip and Bett were given their instructions, and guided a bemused Dolly back to her field.

Poor Daisy though was another problem. Neither Bill's powers of persuasion, nor the power of his muscles would shift her.

"Hadaway and seek Geordie and Tom 'o' Barrowborn lassie, I need a bit hand." Puffed Bill. I needed no second bidding and ran like the wind on my errand.

As I rounded Barrowburn house end, I was thankful to see Granda's little "Fergie" tractor in the yard, and, leaning on his stick, Granda himself, Sheddles in attendance, talking to Geordie and Tom.

"Granda, Daisy's stuck in the dipper and uncle Bill sent me to get help" I panted, red faced and breathless from the run and the excitement of the occasion. Tom slid his cap onto the back of his head and scratched his sparsely covered pate. Geordie hitched his trousers up and hefted his stick, ready for action.

"Right little maid, climb aboard" said Granda, patting the dish shaped tractor seat. I clambered up and we roared off up the road, followed by Sheddles, with Geordie and Tom in hot pursuit, sticks clicking in unison and steel capped tackety boots striking sparks from the road in their unaccustomed haste.

The party reassembled once more round Daisy in her pit.

"Well I go to hell!" Said Geordie in tones of wonder "Hoo did she get doon yonder?"

"It was me," I announced proudly. Uncle Bill explained, amidst loud mooing, hoots of laughter, much knee slapping and head scratching. Nana bustled into the house to make tea for our guests and discussions began as to how to extricate Daisy from her predicament. I sat on the fence and watched, with interest, several abortive attempts to achieve this, until frustration began to colour their language. At this point, Nana returned to haul me unwillingly back to the house.

Later I heard the sound of the Fergie's engine, anguished moo's and loud calls of "Howay! Keep gannin, that's it." And finally, a whoop "She's oot ye bugger!"

I never did find out how they managed it, but the tale of my game of cowboys and its consequences was a source of hilarity for some time to come.

Chapter Six - Eggs and Kylies

You rarely see free-range hens nowadays, but up the valley we would never have dreamed of cooping up the hens. They had complete freedom to range far and wide and they took full advantage of it. The Khaki Campbell ducks too, great favourites of mine, waddled in comical convoy down to the Coquet, which was their highway, dabbling and quacking for miles up and down stream. All our feathered residents returned at feeding times though, and in the evenings, to their roosts, where they were locked in each night, the only time their freedom was restricted.

This freedom must have been idyllic for them, but it did have its drawbacks for us. They had a tendency to lay their eggs all over the place. Very rarely did they drop their cargo in the comfortable nesting boxes provided. These were complete with china (or boody) eggs, installed to show them what was expected, but did they oblige? Not they! A favourite repository was the hayshed, in little hollows in the soft sweet hay. That was not so bad, it was an easy task to find the eggs there, but the more adventurous, or plain awkward chuckies, would walk for miles to find an unlikely or inaccessible place in which to deposit their treasure.

Therefore, it was that one of my summer jobs was to collect the eggs. The first time I was entrusted with this task, I, not unnaturally, headed for the hen house. I thought I'd got a grand haul, until I handed my basket of gleaming white eggs to Nana I still blush at the memory of her mirth as she pointed out to me that these were the "boody" eggs, put in the nests to give the hens the right idea.

Through time though, I became quite adept at spotting the odd hen sneaking away from a likely spot with an assumed casual air, and my ears became attuned to the shrieks of triumph with which they advertised their achievement to the world.

It was on one such egg hunting expedition that I almost failed. I would set off with old Sheddles, Granda's Border collie, for company, and was searching the dyke backs of a hillside just up the road.

<u>**Sheddles and I**</u>

I was enjoying myself. It was a fine day, and Granda had rented this particular hill to someone's herd of highland cattle, or Kylies, as they were known. (I have never understood the modern fashion for calling little girls Kylie!) They were picturesque beasts, ("Varra picturesqueak", old Tom 'o' Barrowburn called them) with flowing coats and magnificent horns. Their colours too were lovely, ranging from reddish-brown through to palest gold. Even better, they had calves with them, appealing, sturdy little things, as cuddly as teddy bears. I loved to look at them, though, unlike our milk cow, Dolly, they were shy and veered away if I got too close.

I wandered along by the wall, alternately scanning its base for likely nesting places and gazing, with pleasure at the beautiful animals.

One calf, a golden creature of great charm, caught my eye. He was irresistible, so I pulled a handful of grass, hoping to coax him to eat. He seemed tempted and took a few hesitant steps in my direction.

"Come on teddy-kylie," I breathed, and moved slowly towards him. What an achievement it would be to touch one of these lovely creatures. I crept closer. Success was almost within my grasp, when Sheddles pushed me roughly away, and to my astonishment, grabbed my cotton dress in his mouth and began dragging me back towards the wall.

"Give over Sheddles man!" I protested; as he pulled me right to the wall and began nudging me up onto its top. I was disappointed at being foiled, and very cross with Sheddles, until I glanced up from his glossy head, to see the calf's mother thundering down the hillside towards me. I was paralysed with fear half way up the wall. Sheddles gave up trying to push me and rounded on the angry cow, which had her horns down and whose intentions clearly were serious.

He barked frantically - a rare thing, since sheep dogs, like shepherds, are not given to wasting words. Running back and forwards in front of the cow, almost between her hooves it seemed he finally stopped her charge and distracted her long enough for me to recover my senses and hurl myself, breathless with relief, over the wall.

The Kylie mother eventually gave up the contest and returned to her calf, which had retreated up the hill. Sheddles leaped the wall like a thoroughbred and sat down, surveying me with his head on one-side ears cocked. His intelligent eyes looked at me more in sorrow than in anger and I could almost hear him saying, "By, you're a daft bairn, look at all the bother you've put me to".

Then he leaned over and slurped his pink tongue comfortingly over my face.

Sheddles and I walked home eggless. He, confidently, his tail waving like a flag. I, on rather unsteady legs, still weak at the thought of my narrow escape.

<u>Walking home eggless</u>

Chapter Seven – The Animals

The animals at Windyhaugh were very much a part of our everyday lives, every bit as important as the people, each one with a well-defined role and individual personality. Teaser for instance, she was Granda's Border Terrier, with the sandy/ginger wiry coat of her breed. Her place was about the house and farm.

Nana with Teaser as a pup

She never accompanied Granda when he ranged further out onto the hills, seeming to know that this was Sheddles' role, but whenever he was within range of the house Teaser was two steps behind him, gazing adoringly up at him, her trusting brown eyes set in a bristly little face. She always sat at his feet in the evening too, but of course during the day Granda was often out on the hill. Then if it was warm Teaser would station herself in some sunny spot in the farmyard where she could doze and keep an eye on the poultry.

Sometimes she temporarily transferred her allegiance to me and trotted along by my side, doing her best to appear enthusiastic about my childish games. The one she liked best was when I made a seesaw out of the "cuddy" or saw horse and an old plank.

When my cousin Alan was at Windyhaugh, we could see-saw away happily for hours and Teaser was content to watch, her head bobbing up and down like one of those little dogs you see in the backs of cars. But, if I was alone, Teaser took on the role of the other half of the seesaw. Of course she was not heavy enough to lift me, but that did not matter. She perched jauntily on her end, ears cocked, and I simply straddled my end, raising and lowering Teaser gently by bending and straightening my legs. She loved it, and if I stopped she yipped at me wagging her short tail until I began again.

Sometimes my legs were aching before Teaser got tired of rising and falling like a liftboy in an elevator.

Teaser was the only animal on the farm that had no real job of work. She was kept simply because Granda loved her. He was something of an authority on Border Terriers, and I remember basking in reflected glory one year at Alwinton Show, when Granda was asked to judge the Border Terrier section.
Tip, Bett and Sheddles, on the other hand, worked extremely hard helping Granda, Bill and Jim with the sheep. They were all Border Collies yet each was slightly different from each other. Tip and Sheddles were rough coated, that is their coats were longer than Bett's. The basic colours of all three were black, with a little white, but Tip had tan eyebrows and little streaks of white around his muzzle. Sheddles had a beautiful black glossy coat with a slight wave to it and a white bib. The prettiest, in my opinion though, was Bett, she was smooth coated, mainly black with white underneath, and just above the edge of her black nose was a little pink patch, (to show that she was a girl, I thought.)

All three were highly intelligent and obedient to the slightest word or whistle. Tip was a fairly dour character, probably because he was the oldest. Sheddles was the brightest, I think, but Bett was graceful and feminine in her movements, gentle and affectionate around the farm, fleet of foot on the hill, a beautiful dog and the most loving.

When she produce a litter of plump black and white pups, she was a wonderful mother. I would like to have to have taken one of her puppies home to Newcastle, but Bett's offspring were bred to be working sheepdogs, and Granda explained to me that they wouldn't be happy living in a town. The herding instinct is strong, and if frustrated finds other outlets. The number of town reared collies I have since seen chasing cars, at great risk to themselves and drivers, would suggest that Granda was right.

My friend, Dante, the farm cat, gave the appearance of being a lady of leisure, slinking elegantly about the house and the farm, but she had an important part to play too. The part which her feline ancestors have played for generations, that of rodent controller. Dante's pretty exterior hid a killer instinct when mice were around, or anything resembling a mouse. She even had designs on the two ferrets, which Granda kept at one time, that's optimism for you.

With me she was long suffering, allowing me to kit her out in my doll's clothes, or playful, when I swung bits of paper on a string for her to catch, or affectionate, when she rubbed around my ankles or purred on my knee, or matey, when we conspired together to keep the hiding places of her latest kittens a secret from Granda. With Granda she was charming and obsequious, especially when he was milking Dolly. With Uncle Bill, who she adored, she was, well, adoring. She didn't care for Uncle Jim though, probably because he didn't care for her, not being a cat lover.

Nana she did the honour of treating as an equal. Both of them were busy ladies with families to attend to. (Intermittently in Dante's case.) She was, when I think of it the only animal that had the run of the house, the farm and the hill, in fact Dante went wherever she wished to, and appeared to have complete control of her own destiny. She was the only animal, I think, who could have survived quite nicely if every human being vanished from the face of the earth. I would love to know how she got the better of the two ferrets though.

The ferrets lived in a cage at one end of the farmyard, and Dante would sit for hours in front of it, fixing them with a malevolent stare and lashing her tail from side to side. Had the ferrets been free, they would no doubt have been the death of her, but since they were behind bars Dante was supremely confident. This state of undeclared warfare between cat and ferrets was what I left behind me at the end of one summer holiday.

On my return the following year, I was of course interested to see how the situation had developed. Initial greetings over, I ran across to the ferret cage to see how the land lay. No sign of Dante crouching before it. I peered through the wires into the dark interior, but could not see the ferrets either. In my efforts to see into the dark recesses of the cage I bumped against the door, slowly it swung open. Deciding to go for broke I reached, inch by inch, carefully into the back of the cage. Right at the back my hand encountered a soft furry body. Not the whippy, vibrant body of a ferret though. This had the soft feel of a contented animal at rest. I groped around and then heard the unmistakable sound—a cross between a purr and a miaow, which Dante kept exclusively for her kittens. Then the sandpaper feel of her tongue rasping gently over my fingers.
Dante's face emerged from the gloom, her green eyes glowed softly and she rubbed her head against my cheek. I felt inside the cage again and encountered small warn furry bodies.

Dante had given birth to her kittens in the ferrets' cage! I lifted one of them out. It was a pretty tabby, eyes just beginning to open, but there was something wrong with the little thing, it had no tail. I replaced it carefully and lifted out another, tortoiseshell and white this time, like its mother but again, no tail. There were five kittens in all four of them without tails. The only complete one was a little ginger kitten, the smallest of the lot. I replaced them carefully and stroked Dante, my eyes blurred with tears. I blundered back into the house weeping noisily.

"Now then little maid, what ist?" asked Granda hauling me onto his lap. "Wheesht, wheesht now and tell your Granda what's wrong."

"Dante's kittens Granda," I sobbed, "The ferrets have bitten their tails off."

" Ferrets! What ferrets?" asked Granda looking puzzled.

“Your ferrets Granda.” I sobbed accusingly, “The ones in the cage, they’ve bitten the tails off all Dante’s kittens bar one.”
“Show yer Granda. Ye ken fine that yer Granda’ll fettle it.” He said soothingly. I wanted Granda to put things right, but was ever mindful of the battle of wits which he and Dante waged. She had to keep her kittens hidden until their eyes were open. If they were discovered before that stage, they got no further. I suppose that Granda was only trying to keep the number of farm cats down to manageable proportions, but Dante didn’t see it that way, so I hesitated before disclosing their hiding place.

“Their eyes are open mind Granda.” I sobbed anxiously.
“Aye well little maid, if they’re wee cats already them Dante’ll likely want to keep them, tails or no.”

Thus reassured I took Granda’s hand and led him to the ferrets’ cage.
“The crafty little divil, aah would nivvor o’ thowt to look for them here...” he said, as he stooped down to peer into the gloom. His large hand plunged into the depths of the cage and emerged again cradling a miniature of Dante, minus tail.
“Bye, she’s as like her mam as makes nee odds, bar the tail.” He said softly.
“But Granda, why have the ferrets eaten the tails?” I wailed in anguish
“There, there little maid, the ferrets haven’t eaten their tails at all. Thor ferrets haven’t been here for months, I got shot o’ the little divils last autumn.” I digested this news with amazement.
“Well what’s happened to the kittens’ tails Granda? Where have they gone?”
“Well it’s like this maidie, thor kittens has a Manx cat for a dad, and Manx cats has nee tails. Ye see how thor kitten is the same colour as her mam?”
“Yes” I said calming down.

"Well she's the same shape as her dad, and so are the other three, but thor kitten," he said holding the ginger one with the tail, "it's the same shape as her mam."

Dante reared her family safely in the home vacated by her enemies, and from then on there was always a Manx cat of one colour or another among Nana and Granda's complement of cats.

An interesting postscript concerns the ginger kitten. Ginger cats are always supposed to be toms, or at least barren if they are queens. This ginger cat was both a queen and fertile, she proved it time and again over the years to come.

Sally the sow produced litters too. Her young were every bit as appealing as the kittens, silky skinned squirming piglets with shrill demanding voices. How Sally did not crush the little things as her huge bulk flopped down among them I'll never know. She didn't though, each piglet scrambled safely to its appointed nipple to feed, while Sally grunted her contentment. None of the piglets ever looked like their mum. Sally's black and white colouring was arranged in an orderly fashion, black at either end, with a band of white (pale pink to be exact) around her middle.

She seemed to have slap dash way of colouring her piglets though; they were always pink with black spots splattered over them any old how.

I didn't see as much of Dick, the carthorse, as I did the other animals, because in summer, he spent most of his time in the field up the hill.

He worked very hard in hay making time, hauling loads of hay from field to stack yard, but apart from that and the occasional load of stuff to be delivered about the valley, he seemed to have a quite a cushy time of it.

He was a huge creature, a lovely chestnut colour, with feathery circles of hair around his ankles, and enormous feet. Although I knew that Dick was slow and gentle, I found his size rather intimidating until my Uncle Bill called out one day, " howay lassie, de ye want a ride te Bygate in the keart?"

I'd never heard Bygate mentioned before, so it was the attraction of visiting a new place, rather than the ride in the cart which made me gladly agree and follow Uncle Bill to where Dick was patiently waiting to begin the journey.

I was hoisted up onto the cart, and made myself comfortable among the sacks bursting with cargo that was Bygate bound. Bill flipped the reins, and off we went. Dick's massive hindquarters had an hypnotic quality, as he plodded over the road bridge passed Barrowburn, and the dance hall and then took a cart track leading into the hills. I can't understand how I'd never noticed this track before; it began quite near where mam and I got off the bus. I sat up and looked around with interest. As we climbed higher we had a wonderful view of Windyhaugh and Barrowburn, an angle I'd never seen them from before, then we went over the hilltop, and they were gone. Instead, before us was a vista of hilltops speckled with sheep.

"So this is where they get to," I thought.

The track eventually led to a ruin, which looked to me then that of a very large house, almost a mansion, although what a mansion would be doing up there I have no idea. Everything looks larger to a child, so perhaps it was just the ruin of another hill farm. I have never been back to check, so it retains an air of mystery in my mind.

Uncle Bill unloaded the sacks into a tumble down outbuilding, while Dick cropped lazily at the tufts of grass between the heather. "Right Lorna doon and up again," says Bill. "Are ee ganna drive back?"

"Me!" I squeaked, "I canna drive a horse n' cart."

"Course ye can. There's nowt te it. Sit ye doon here and get a hadden o' the reins. If ye want Dick te gan straight aheed, just leave well enough alain. If ye want te torn right, just give a bit tweak on the rein on the right side, and if ye want te gan left, twitch the rein on the other side."
"What do I do if I want to make him go backwards?"
Uncle Bill looked at me in exasperation "What the hell wad ye want te gan backwards for? Howay, tak the reins and aah'll keep ye right."
I took the reins nervously, Uncle Bill shouted, "Git up there" and off we went.

What power! I tried Dick out, just to see if he really would go the way the reins told him to, and he actually obeyed my commands. Consequently we wove our way home as though Dick had had one too many. I must say that Uncle Bill was very forbearing. A wry smile was all that gave away his opinion of our convoluted journey. We must have covered twice as much ground on the way back as we did on the way there! As a result of it though, I lost my slight nervousness of Dick's size. After all, I reasoned, if all it took to control him was the twitch of the reins in the hand of a child, he must be a big softy.

Every farm up the valley had a house cow, sometimes two, to provide milk for the household. They were usually shorthorns, a breed you see little of now. Slow, stolid animals, with a built in time clock, which told them unerringly when it was time for them to queue up for milking. They were such placid creatures that even the shy wild rabbits hopped among their feet without fear.

Occasionally, motherless lambs were hand reared and these "pet" lambs were normally kept in a paddock close to the house. On one of my visits I formed a close relationship with a pet lamb, so much so that he followed me all over the farm and we were inseparable. However, the evil day eventually dawned when it was time for him to go off to the mart with the other lambs. I found this out quite by chance when I overheard uncle Jim discussing it with Granda.

Once the initial shock of this revelation had faded, my mind turned frantically to ways of rescuing my pet from this fate. I'd have to hide him, but where?

The answer came when my eye lit on the old disused dry toilet, or netty. This one was practically a ruin, unlike the one in Granda's garden which was still serviceable.

It had no door, but the wooden compartment, the "business" end was still intact. I lifted the lid and peered into the black pit.

Disused or not, it was not an inviting prospect. Still, "needs must" I clutched the wriggling lamb round the middle and struggled with him, trying to calm his plaintive bleats, down into the depths of the netty.

Reaching up, I hauled the wooden lid along so that it more or less covered the hole. Lamb and I settled back in the dark to wait it out. Once the lorry with the other lambs had left for Rothbury mart, we'd be safe, so it was just a matter of time.

It worked too! Granda and uncle Jim did eventually find us, when Lamb (he never was blessed with a proper name) became hungry for his overdue feed and began to bleat. Our discovery was greeted with much relief and laughter, and to my delight, Lamb had indeed missed his lift to the mart and continued to be my close companion for the rest of that summer.

Lamb and I

Although I was aware of the wild inhabitants of the valley, I was not of course on such familiar terms with them as with the domestic animals. I regularly saw foxes, rabbits, weasels and stoats, as well as various birds, so I thought I knew all the valley's inhabitants, even those less frequently encountered. It came as a complete shock therefore, when I heard one year that the Blindburn folk had made a pet of a wild goat kid, so I couldn't wait to see it.

I was spending that summer with Aunty Bett and Uncle Bill at Rowhope, so we set off to Blindburn to visit her parents and the goat. On the way we stopped to exchange a friendly word or two with a gang of roadmen who were painting one of the metal bridges, which took the road over the river Coquet. At Blind burn, Bett was soon in animated conversation with her mother, while I was straight outside to see the latest acquisition. I was not disappointed; the little goat was absolutely charming. His shaggy coat was black and white and he had two budding horns on his forehead. He skipped around me playfully and butted my hands to see if I had brought anything to eat. The time flew by, so I was surprised when Aunty Bett called me for the return journey to Rowhope.

We didn't see the roadmen on the way back as they had finished the bridge, we remarked on how smart it looked with its new coat of paint and dismissed it from our minds.

A few days later, however, we had cause to remember it again. The sad news came from Blindburn, that the little goat was dead. He had licked the newly painted bridge and died of lead poisoning. Thankfully people now realise the danger of lead in paint, but too late for the wild goat kid.

Lorna had a little lamb.

Lorna had a little lamb
Or so I have been told
I really can't remember
'Cos I wasn't very old

I have a faded photograph
In shades of black and white
It shows a lassie and her lamb
So the story must be right

I fed him and I petted him
And sheltered him from harm
He followed me around the place
Upon my Granda's farm

Then one day in my wanderings
I heard my uncle say
"The lassie's lamb will hev te gan
To Rothbury mart today"

Such a thing could never be
I'd have to hide my pet
My uncle Jim was after him
But he hadn't got him yet!

I toddled down the garden path
And opened up the door
Of an ancient outside netty
That I'd never used before

I lifted up the wooden lid
And gazed into the pit
It didn't look a pleasant place
For a lamb and I to sit

But in we climbed and shut the lid
And huddled in the dark
A little lassie and her lamb
Who didn't want to part

"Where the hells that lassie gone"
I heard my uncle say
"I haven't seen hor or that lamb
Since early on today"

"I never thought she'd lead me
On such a merry dance
The lorry's leaving shortly
So the lamb'll miss its chance"

Any minute now and we'd
Be able to come out
Then I' have to face my uncle
'Cos I knew that he would shout

I heard the welcome sound
Of uncle Jim's retreating feet
But by then my lamb decided
On that very time to bleat

"What's that?" I heard him saying
"I thought I heard a lamb"
I'd lifted up the netty lid
But shut it with a slam

"By gum ye naughty lassie
D' ye want your backside hit?
If ye diven't fetch that lamb back now
Ye'll be right in the sh..!

"I think she's maybe in it now"
My Granda, laughing said
"That sound came from the netty
In the old dry toilet shed"

They lifted up the netty lid
And much to their surprise
From the depths of the old toilet
Gazed back two pairs of eyes

We both were lifted out of it
While Jim and Granda laughed
And Nana filled the tin bath
And the pair of us were bathed

Upon the following morning
He was waiting at the gate
But you know, I can't remember
That lamb's eventual fate
(Just as well)

Chapter Eight - Parcels and Visitors.

Visitors from outside the valley were rare in those days, before car ownership was common. One regular visitor however, was the mail carrier. He was our link with the outside world and fulfilled one of the roles of the peddler in medieval times, in that he spread news and gossips up and down the valley. He also gave the occasional lift, passed verbal messages from farm to farm and performed many valuable services to the community, over and above the one for which the Post Office employed him.

The red Royal Mail van went past every morning about ten 'o' clock. We always exchanged cheery waves, but sometimes the van turned off over the metal Road Bridge and came right up to the house. Usually it would just be to deliver the "Farmers Weekly", or a bill or two, but sometimes it was a letter, and once it was a parcel for me!

That particular year, I had been allowed to plant seeds in a small patch of our garden, back in Newcastle, but my summer visit to Windyhaugh meant that I'd had to leave them half grown.

When the mail carrier drove up that day, he held out a letter and a large, flat, cardboard box, tied up with lots of string. The letter was for Nana, but the postman asked with mock solemnity,

"Is there a Miss Lorna Elizabeth Nairn in residence?" and when I owned up, handed the parcel to me! I had never received a parcel through the post in my life! I was astonished, puzzled and very excited - torn between the desire to see what was in it and the desire to savour every moment of opening my very own parcel.

I began, carefully; to unpick the knots, but Uncle Bill, as curious as I and more impatient, opened the little knife he kept for trimming sheep's feet, and waded in. "Howay woman! You're ganna be on all bloody day at that rate and aah want Te be back te the hill before the morn's morn."

He cut the last strings and hovered over me as I lifted the lid.

Inside, carefully wrapped in tissue paper, was an armful of summer flowers. Marigolds, Snapdragons, Cornflowers and all the other results of the packet of mixed seeds I had planted in the spring.

My mother had picked them for me and sent them, so that I should not miss the fruits of my labour. I have received many a parcel since that day, but none, which has given me more pleasure.

My parcel

The letter turned out to be exciting too. It was from Aunty Peg, to say that she would be bringing my cousin Alan, a few months younger than I, to stay for a while at Windyhaugh. Aunty Peg, Nana and Granda's daughter, was a great favourite of mine.

She loved children, and Alan eventually had six brothers and sisters, all brought up on Northumbrian hill farms, where their father worked as a shepherd.

At that time though, Alan was an only child. A blonde little devil of a boy, who, like me, loved to come to Windyhaugh.

Preparations were put in hand immediately to make ready for our guests. They were to arrive with the next day's post van, so there was no time to waste.

In those days the post van often carried unofficial passengers to isolated areas. Now the Post Office has regularised the situation by running a post bus up the valley.

Windyhaugh had three bedrooms upstairs.
Downstairs, was the scullery, with its walk-in pantry, the farm kitchen, which was the hub of the house, and the front room, which as far as I could tell, was kept just for show.

There was no bathroom. We washed in the scullery and bathed in a long tin bath in front of the fire. The toilet was a dry closet in the garden, and every bed had a chamber pot lurking beneath it.

Nana and Granda had one bedroom, Bill and Jim had another and I had the little front bedroom with a view back down the valley towards Barrowburn and the tiny school perched on the hillside beyond.

Nana had decided that Aunty Peg and I would share a bed for the few days of her stay, and Alan would sleep in Bill and Jim's room, which, on the face of it, wouldn't seem to necessitate much reorganisation.

However, the prospect of visitors arriving seemed to galvanise Nana into action.

Every mat in the house was hauled out and shaken, if it was small enough. Larger ones were hung over the washing line and walloped soundly with the carpet beater.

Linoed floors were thoroughly swept and Nana would hurl the resulting shovelfuls of dust and fluff into the fire with satisfaction, saying, "That's one pile 'o' muck will bother me nee mair!".

I was entrusted with dusting the musty front room and polishing the huge mahogany sideboard, resplendent with many mirrors and ledges.

I took the job very seriously and was careful to return the china dogs, family photographs and innumerable nick knacks to their exact positions.

The family photographs were fascinating. There was one of five pretty girls that Nana told me were her nieces in Western Australia, one of her sisters having emigrated there as a newly married young woman.

There was also a picture of a lovely dark eyed lady, a mysterious figure, whom I later learned was Granda's mother. She, we were told, had been the daughter of landed gentry on the Scottish side of the border, near Kelso.

She had fallen for, and unusually for those times, actually married, my great grandfather, who was a gamekeeper on her family estate, and a widower with four children. However, soon after giving birth to Granda, the novelty of being a gamekeeper's wife apparently wore off and she retreated to the "big house", abandoning her husband and child. Being unable to cope with the small baby, great grandfather farmed him out to relatives in Northumberland, which is why Granda was reared a Northumbrian, rather than a Scot.

I can't imagine how she must have felt, leaving her baby. I wonder if she ever thought about him over the years. She must have had a certain amount of conscience though, because, until he died, Granda received a small annuity which I believe came from his mother's family.

The picture of the five girls stayed in my memory too. So much so, that I made efforts to contact them in later years. This led to visits between the two long parted branches of the family one of the girls came with her husband to visit the land of their ancestors, fell in love with Northumberland, and repeated the visit many times since. The son of another of the girls became the Australian white water canoeing champion, and visited us every time he competed in Europe. Little did I realise the repercussions dusting those photographs would have on so many lives, years later!

With hindsight, Nana probably gave me that job to keep me out from under her feet, while she got on with the real work. Sheets were changed, feather mattresses plumped, and an ingenious carved wooden chair which unfolded into a bed, was made up for Alan.
Granda, meanwhile, had busied himself erecting a tall thin shed of corrugated iron down by the river; there was much hammering, banging and swearing and the finished article looked like a tin coffin stood on end. It crossed my mind to wonder what it was, but I was confident that Granda wouldn't have undertaken the task without good reason, so I didn't ask.

Chapter Nine - The Netty

The day dawned cloudy, but the post van brightened the morning by dropping Aunty Peg, Alan and a large parcel at the end of the bridge. I rushed out to meet them, and Alan, racing past me in the opposite direction, aimed a playful punch as he went. Aunty Peg, slowed down by the heavy parcel, called, "Hallow their bonny lass. How's yersel?"
Aunty Peg was a warm person, quick to laugh, and it gladdened my heart to see her.

Aunty Peg

Once in the house, Peg and Nana set to talking and arguing straight away, so Alan and I went outside to play.

Somehow, the pace of life was quicker when Alan was there. No reflective wanderings, no time for contemplation. Trouble straight away' within minutes, Alan had found a rope and by dint of much puffing, panting and hurling, he had it slung over a beam in the hay shed. There, he played Tarzan, swinging like an erratic pendulum, frightening hens and kittens by leaping down into the piles of soft hay, yelling at the top of his voice.

The parcel had been claimed by Granda, and he vanished with it in the direction of his new shed.

Dinner over, he rose to his feet with an air of importance.
"Wee's ganna be the forst te try the new netty then?" He asked.

Everyone looked at him questioningly.

"Aah've built ye a new netty doon bi the born, and the postie fetched the chemical toilet te gan in it this mornin', so howay, wee' ganna volunteer?"

"Aah will Granda," shouted Alan, half way out of the house already.

We all followed and watched, as Granda lifted the little hook, which fastened the door and ushered him inside.

Alan vanished into the gloom, closing the door behind him, but not before I had noticed the squares of torn up Farmer's Weekly pages hanging on a string from a nail. So, it wasn't that different from the dry toilet, I thought. The Farmers Weekly was certainly indispensable up the valley, Nana, Granda, Aunty Peg, Bill, Jim and I hovered outside expectantly. In a minute or two, Alan emerged.

"Well?" Asked Granda.

"Champion!" pronounced Alan emphatically. So, the new netty passed the test.

"Netty" is believed by some to be a corruption of the word, necessary, and of course, it was, both for the purposes of nature and as a refuge. I once hid a pet lamb, which was due to go to the mart, in the old netty for almost a whole day, while uncle Jim searched high and low for it. (Chapter 7)

The old netty was a grand place to think, and to dream too. It was stone built, with a wooden door, which had a gap top and bottom, and three holes drilled at about adult's eye level.

The seating arrangement was a plank with a hole in it and toilet rolls were unheard of. Squares of shiny paper from the Farmers Weekly served that purpose.

Once in a while, a Northumberland Gazette, or a Newcastle Journal found it's way there, and if you got one of their mat finished absorbent pages, you counted yourself lucky.

At home, in Newcastle, we had a flush toilet, albeit at the end of the yard, but I preferred the Windyhaugh netty. It had an air of sanctuary quite lacking in the one at home.

The Barrow burn netty, however, was a cut above even that, it was "a sociable" a two seater. It's plank boasted two holes, with a space between for playing cards!

Almost as Alan emerged from the new toilet, the clouds, which had heralded the day, began to unburden themselves of their cargo of rain. It was back to the house for us.

Granda, Bill and Jim had to work to occupy them in the farm buildings, Nana and Peg busied themselves in the scullery, so Alan and I sat ourselves on the wide windowsill with a pile of the ubiquitous Farmers Weeklies and leafed through them for the few pictures they contained. The bright yellow cover page was pretty boring, and to be frank, so was the rest of it for a couple of five year olds, so we abandoned them in favour of a pair of hen's feet. (We had eaten the rest of the hen for dinner) We chased each other around the kitchen, pulling at the exposed tendons to make the feet curl and uncurl like talons.

The rain continued to pour down heavily, the Coquet was rising rapidly, and within a short time, it was a roaring torrent. Eventually, the men folk retreated to the house, and shaking water from their caps, stood steaming in front of the fire.

"Bloody awful weather ye've fetched wi' ye Peg" called Jim.
"Aye, well a bit rain'l no hort ye." Answered Peg, preoccupied with helping Nana in the scullery.

"Aah wanna gan Te the netty Granda. " Alan announced suddenly

"Just use the jerry son." Granda advised.

Alan squirmed and looked embarrassed. "No, aah think aah really need the netty,"

"Bloody hell!" Said Bill. "Of all the times to be caught short! Right in the middle of the worst storm of the year. Here y'are, put this roond ye, and hadaway Te the new netty, it's nearest.

Bill swathed Alan in a huge oilskin cape, and off he went, into the storm. In a very short time, he was back, looking rather shocked.

"The netty's gone." He said, "It's away doon the born."
After a moments silence, while we digested this news, Peg and Bill burst into raucous laughter, and soon we were all laughing. Except Alan. "But aah still need the netty!" He wailed.
"Hout! the poor bairn," said Nana. "Howay son. Ye'll hetta gan te the aad yin doon the garden."

And so it was that the usurper was demolished, and the old netty reinstated to its rightful position.

<u>**The New Netty**</u>

Sweating and heaving and grunting with strain
Granda was working outside in the rain
Building a shed of some sort was the task
I wondered what for and decided to ask

"That's our new netty" my Granda replied
(Their home still had not got a toilet inside)
"The old one is getting beyond it I doubt
And this one is closer, although it is still out"

We quickly admired it then dashed back inside
And hung our wet coats by the fire where they dried
Nana was baking and Alan would draw
I stared out the window and here's what I saw

Soaking wet sheep up on the hill
Rain from the gutters beginning to spill
Puddles were everywhere spreading around
The River was rising fast covering more ground

Suddenly Alan said, "I'll have to go
And test the new netty, or else use the po."
"Put on your coat lad and outside you get,"
Said Nana, "There's no need for using pos yet"

"The rain isn't that bad, your skin's waterproof
And the new netty has a good watertight roof"
Outside he ran in his wellies and mac
But it wasn't that long before Alan came back

"Where's the new netty gone Granda," he cried
"What do ye mean son?" my Granda replied
Hastily we donned our coats and looked out
Our lovely new netty was nowhere about

Puzzled my Granda stood scratching his head
Nana was pointing, "It's there, look," she said
Away down the river, a little brown boat
Went Granda's new netty completely afloat

We watched it in silence as it sailed away
The old netty would live to see a new day
Alan sighed sadly, "I still never tried it,
But I'll think myself lucky I wasn't inside it."

The Netty

Chapter Ten - The River.

The weeks sped by. Happy hours could be spent collecting chickweed for the hens. This killed two birds with one stone -helping to clear Granda's garden of the creeping Bird's eye Speedwell, and providing a treat for the hens, who loved it. (Perhaps that is why it is called "chickweed!") Periodically, the hens were also fed on crushed up old crockery, (boody, Nana called it), or even their own crushed up eggshells. Nana told me this was to ensure that they laid eggs with good, hard shells. After one feed of crushed up Willow Pattern, I examined the eggs for weeks, looking for one with the distinctive blue and white pattern, but to no avail.

Damming the Coquet

There was always plenty to do - nests to be made among the reeds by the riverbank, for instance. I hoped that some wild creature would be glad of the residences I so carefully constructed for them.

I selected circular clumps of reeds, flattened the middle to make a hollow and bound the tops of the outside reeds together. The banks of the Coquet often looked like a miniature Indian settlement, with its scattering of little reed tepees. The inescapable fact that nothing ever moved into them didn't discourage me in the slightest. I was an optimistic child.
The river was a great attraction of course. It was very shallow in most places, so we could plodge about among the rocks with perfect safety. Alan was a great one for building dams, so the pair of us would heave stones about happily for hours, trying, unsuccessfully to stop the Coquet in its tracks. The most we achieved was a slight hold up and a fractional increase in the depth of the water behind our ramshackle wall.

One such pool came in handy though. Nana had set a clutch of duck eggs under a clocker (a broody hen). Clockers were strange creatures, quite unlike their sisters. They entered into a trance like state, fluffing their feathers up and staying put on their nest of eggs, no matter what.

The result of the most recent clockers endeavours was a clutch of bantam chicks, appealing little mites, but even they couldn't compete for charm with the duck eggs when they hatched. Their foster mother was extremely proud of them, seeming not to notice their webbed feet, rounded beaks and reedy attempts to quack. She paraded her waddling flotilla of offspring endlessly around the farmyard to show them off, but Alan and I noticed that she never took them near the river.

"Ye knaw, thor little ducks is never ganna lam te swim." Remarked Alan thoughtfully one day. That was it! We decided that something had to be done, and our latest dammed up pool was just the place. Amidst panic stricken clucking from their foster mum, we captured the ducklings and wheeled them down to the river in my doll's pram with mother hen in hot pursuit.

I lifted each fluffy bundle carefully out, webbed feet flailing, and placed them at the waters edge. Alan meanwhile, plodged out into the water, quacking encouragement. The ducklings, reluctant at first, soon got the idea and launched themselves, little bits of flotsam on the water. Mother hen was frantic, to see her darlings in the river and ran up and down the bank, wild eyed and clucking. The ducklings organised themselves into formation, and piping their pleasure with reedy little voices, swam round and round the pool, doing their best to avoid Alan and I who were in there with them. They ignored their mother completely. I'll bet they got what for when she finally retrieved them and led them; stiff legged with anger, back to the farmyard.

Kidnapping the Ducks

There was one deep pool in our part of the river. It lay alongside the backfield, behind the hayshed, and I avoided it. Not from any fear of drowning, but from an uneasy suspicion that a monster could easily lie hidden in its dark depths. I hadn't read about the troll in "The Three Billy Goats Gruff" for nothing!

One particularly hot day, uncle Bill paused in his labours, and hefting the tin bath onto his shoulders, called out," Howay ee two bairns and aah'l take ye for a ride on the river.
We scampered along behind him, delighted to have uncle Bill to play with. Through the stackyard and across the back field we went. Past Daisy and Dolly, who lifted their heads and followed our progress with wondering eyes.

A little doubt began to niggle at the corner of my mind when I realised where we were heading. Uncle Bill was unmistakably making for the black, brooding pool. I faltered in mid skip and hung back. A tussle began in my mind, half of me thinking, "Its only the Coquet, the same water I play in further downstream in the shallows, and uncle Bill would never take me anywhere dangerous". The other half of me fluttering with illogical fear of the dark water, and what could be lurking beneath it.

I reached the riverbank in time to see uncle Bill lower the bath into the water. There was a rope fastened to the handle at one end.
"Here, keep a hadden that son" he said, handing it to Alan. Then, stripping down to his shorts, to my horror, he dived straight into the dark depths. For a moment he looked like a large pale fish through the brackish water. Then he broke the surface, shaking water from his black hair, and laughing up at us.

"Howay then hoy us the rope Alan."

Alan obediently hoyed the rope and Bill pulled the bath to the side.
"Climb aboard ye two and aah'll give ye a tow."

Alan needed no further invitation and stepped into the bath, which settled a little lower in the water. I was horrified. There was no way I could back out without appearing a silly, cowardly girl, so I bit the bullet and gingerly stepped off the solid safe river bank, into the wildly rocking vessel. I sat down; teeth clenched and knuckles white where I gripped the sides of the bath. I tried not to think of what was beneath me through the thin sheet of metal, as we set off.

Uncle Bill swam round that pool for what felt like hours, never seeming to tire. Alan loved it. He knelt in the front whooping with glee and using his hands as paddles to help the bath along. Eventually, I plucked up the courage to let go with one hand and dip it, hesitantly into the water. It was cold and tinted brown with peat, but nothing bit my fingers. I began to relax. If only Alan would Sit still and stop rocking the bath, it would really be quite pleasant.

I leaned back against the edge, my hand trailing idly in the river. Alan chose that precise moment to leap to his feet in excitement.

"Yonder's a salmon!" he shrieked.

The rope was yanked from uncle Bill's hand, as the bath flipped over backwards, ducking me and catapulting Alan into the river. I plummeted down through a silent brown world, then, up I bounced, back into the light, spluttering and splashing. Uncle Bill grasped the neck of my frock and hauled me to the bank, where I sat, as miserable as a wet hen. Alan had landed near the bank, and scrambled out unaided, laughing uproariously.

"Are ee all right hinny?" asked uncle Bill, torn between concern for me and the urge to join in Alan's laughter. Was I all right? I decided that I was. I had been right down to the bottom of the dark pool and seen that there was no monster. I beamed with relief, and soon the three of us were rolling about the riverbank like wet puppies, helpless with laughter.

I was never afraid of the dark pool again.

Chapter Eleven – Nana

Sometimes, if I was up early enough, I went With Granda and Sheddles to look the sheep. We always took the cart track, which led, up the hill behind the house first. About fifty yards up, the ground more or less levelled out into a small field hanging over the valley. This was where Dick, the placid, chestnut coloured carthorse usually grazed and it was the best field for mushrooms on the farm. I became adept at spotting them, ranging over the field far ahead of Granda in my quest. Sometimes, I was disappointed, when the glint of white turned out to be a puffball. I could never resist kicking them to watch them disintegrate in a cloud of smoky innards.

Granda's cheviots and little black-faced sheep had to "looked" twice a day. There were beess to care for as well. (Beess, being the collective name given to the store cattle being fattened for market.) The work of the farm was divided amongst Granda, Bill and Jim. The two milkings a day were shared too. Granda doing the honours in the morning, on his return from the hill, and Nana seeing to the evening session. This evening commitment seemed to weigh heavily on her though. She could be heard, anxiously murmuring at regular intervals throughout the day, "Aah'll hetta milk thor coos, aah'll hetta milk thor coos", so that when milking time actually arrived, she was exhausted, just thinking about it!

Nana's favourite job was seeking sticks. She would walk for miles collecting wood for the fire. In a valley more or less bereft of trees this was no easy task, but she always returned with armfuls of kindling, and on one memorable occasion, half a tree, hauled from the riverbank, where the latest floods had deposited it. The "cuddy" was brought out on which to saw up this prize, and it kept the fire going for days. I was a grown woman before I found out that the correct name for a cuddy was a sawhorse!

I liked accompanying Nana on her wooding quests. About the house and farm she was always busy, but these long walks seemed to relax her and she had time to laugh and talk, though she never lost sight of the purpose behind the walk. Her eyes constantly scanned the landscape. She particularly coveted the recently erected telegraph poles.
"Bye, thor's a grand bit stick." She would say, weighing them up with a practised eye.

I suppose keeping the fire lit was of much more importance then. We tend to take so much for granted now, but in those days, the fire heated water for baths, boiled kettles and pans of potatoes heated the oven and the house, and disposed of much of the rubbish. It was a vital part of the home. The kettle, always on or near the fire, was constantly full of hot water and never far off the boil. Years later, when Nana had electricity at her disposal and an electric kettle was brought into play, she found the wait for it to boil interminable.
"We'll hetta shorten thor flex." she pronounced. I thought her logic was faultless!

Nana was a dab hand with a rabbit pie or a rice pudding. Since seeing my first "mixie" rabbit, I have never been able to bring myself to eat it again. Not even the frozen anonymous carcasses imported from China. In those days though, myxematosis was unheard of and at Windyhaugh, rabbit pie was delicious.

Growing up on the farm, you soon learn to divorce the sight of the living animal from the meal on your plate. I remember my hands and arms being scratched to ribbons by a frantic rabbit that I tried to rescue from the farm dogs. Seeing them alive, I would have done anything to save them. Once they were dead however, that was another matter, and I enjoyed every mouthful. Alan and I used to fight over the choicest pieces, especially the kidneys.

Being ignorant of the science of anatomy, we didn't realise that rabbits had two, and the chances were, with Nana dishing out the portions, we would both get one. Junkets were my favourite pudding, but the rice puddings were delicious too, and filling.

"That'll clag te yer ribs" she would say, dollopping leaden spoonfuls onto our plates. None of your wishy-washy rice pudding swimming in liquid, this was solid stuff with a skin you could dance on. Nana herself was a walking testimonial to the truth of its rib sticking qualities. She was a very large lady, of ample proportions, and when she sat down, her stomach sat on her lap! One of her favourite sayings was "If ye hetta work, ye hetta hev yer meat" and she did! Nana would shift a meal that would have fed two men, but always, as a concession to her weight, she would ostentatiously put saccharin in her tea instead of sugar!

How she managed to chew her meals, I don't know, because Nana never wore her teeth. I didn't notice this absence of molars, until she put them in one day to go visiting relatives.

Her face took on an expression of alert concentration, as though watching for them to leap out of her mouth and her speech was peppered with whistles and hisses.
"What's the matter with you, Nana," I asked, "You're talkin' funny"
Itsss me teethss" she whistled, "They're sssso ssssslack, aah can neither heck nor gee wi' the damned thingssss"
"Well why do you wear them then?" I asked
"Dinna be sssso daft, I canna gan oot te ssssee folk withoot me teethssss! I wadn't be able te sssssmile, and aah canna ssssit all day wi' a glum face and me gob clamped sssssshut!"

The visit was a real ordeal for Nana. She managed to whistle and hiss her way through the conversation, but, I noticed that whenever she flashed her teeth in a smile, she had to tilt her head back at an awkward angle to stop her teeth from falling in her lap Her discomfort became acute, when offered refreshments.

There was no way she could partake of the spread with her wayward teeth in place. I watched, with interest, to see how she would surmount this problem and was surprised to see her produce a large white hankie, apparently to blow her nose. As far as I knew, Nana didn't have a cold, yet the hankie hovered round her face for quite some time until she thought herself unobserved. Then she furtively disgorged the teeth into the hankie and stuffed them quickly down her large bosom! A chancy place to keep them, I thought, but she survived the day unbitten and was able to enjoy the food.

Meals at Windyhaugh were plain fare, but very tasty, potatoes grown on the farm and other vegetables from Granda's garden. Sometimes, Alan and I didn't wait for them to get out of the garden.

Me in the garden

Among other things, Granda grew rows of delicious peas. I wasn't above picking the odd pod and consuming them there on the quiet, but when Alan started devouring them wholesale, I began to worry. I few may not be missed, but Alan's rate of consumption would be bound to give the game away and spoil everything.

"Alan, you'd better not eat any more of me Granda's peas. He's got them all counted ye know." I announced one day with conviction.
"Get away! He canna coont all these." said Alan scornfully, but he hesitated in mid chew, so I knew I'd won. " 'Course he can. You know how Granda counts everything. When he's finished counting the sheep every morning, why do you think he comes into the garden? It's to count the peas. You'd better not eat any more the day, or he's bound to miss them."

"Mebese you're right." Reluctantly, Alan came out from between the rows of peas and raced off to look for entertainment elsewhere. I was silently congratulating my self, when the netty door opened, and out stepped Granda, grinning from ear to ear.
"Bye, yer a grand little maid, looking after yer granda's peas like that" he said, and off he went, chuckling to himself.

My love of garden peas got me into trouble once, and gave Nana a terrible fright.

There was a narrow strip of garden along the front of the house, which had as much wire round it as a concentration camp. Not to keep the flowers in, but to keep the hens and other livestock out. This was Nana's preserve. The most striking flowers in her garden were the lupins. Stately blooms of blues pinks and yellows, but what caught my eye was not their lovely colours. I had noticed that, as the flowers died, little pods appeared. To my eye, they looked exactly the same as the peas in Granda's garden, so, through the gate I went, intent on eating my fill.

The contents of the pods were disappointingly small. Never mind, there were plenty of them; I'd just have to eat more. The taste wasn't up to much either. However, having embarked on a course of action, I wasn't about to give up easily. Perhaps these peas were an acquired taste. Chomping resolutely away at them, I glimpsed Nana through the window, busying herself inside the house. I tapped on the window and gave her a happy wave. Nana smiled and waved back. Then her face froze as she noticed my bulging cheeks. She turned away, giving me a view of her ample rear end as she bustled out of the back door. In a second, she was round at the front of the house, bearing down on me.

"Marcy me lassie! What are ee eating?"

"Just these peas Nana" I mumbled through a half chewed mouthful.
"Hout! Ye daft besom! Thor's not peas, thor's lupin seeds. Spit them oot, quick!"

I obediently emptied my mouth.

"Hoo many mair ha' ye eaten?" She asked urgently
"Just a few Nana. I'm sorry for eatin' your peas. ' I was worried now. Something was obviously very wrong. Nana was pacing up and down the little garden path. With her familiar distress cry, "Marcy me, Noo what'll we dee?"
She seemed to decide, for suddenly, her pacing stopped and she grabbed my hand.
"Howay lassie, I'll hetta make ye hoy up"

I was rushed round the house and in the back door, my feet hardly touching the ground. Before I knew what had hit me, a dose of foul tasting medicine was forced down my throat. It scarcely reached my stomach, before it made the return journey, accompanied by my haul of lupin seeds.

Needless to say, I was as right as rain in a few minutes.

Medicines were fairly basic up the valley, but they did the trick.

Boils or infected sores were "drawn" with a soap and sugar poultice. Goose grease was used for sore throats, and if I fell and grazed my knee, Nana would put peroxide on it.

I don't know if it was the same stuff beloved of many blondes today, but it stung a bit and bubbled on my skin in a very interesting way. Certainly, all my scraped knees mended beautifully.

Nana's garden

Nana had a garden
It was just a narrow band
Behind its fence of chicken wire
This was her own land

She battled to protect it
From marauding hens and ducks
From cats and dogs, pet lambs
And other strokes of rotten luck

Granda used his garden
To grow food for the pot
Things the family needed
Frivolous it was not!

It had a fringe of pansies
And some massive dahlias towered
But its staple crops were onions
Cabbage, peas and cauliflowers

Granda's was important
It was kept behind a wall
Nana's hardly had
Protection there at all

Sweet William, Phlox and Lupins
Bloomed there stubbornly with pride
While Nana beamed with pleasure
Through the window from inside

Granda laboured hard for hours
With spade and fork and hoe
Nana snatched odd moments
When her other work was slow

She kept an eye upon it
As she busied through the day
A bang upon the window
Chased the hens and ducks away

Granda's garden kept us fed
While Nana's, for its part
Cheered the eye with colour
And gladdened every heart

Chapter Twelve - The Hair Cut.

Medicines weren't the only thing administered at home. The nearest barber was in Rothbury, and might as well have been on the moon. Haircuts therefore were home made efforts too. The equipment was kept in a box in the kitchen press. To be precise, on the top shelf, behind the curtained glass doors, along with bags of sugar, salt, bicarbonate of soda and other culinary aids. The three deep drawers below this cupboard, contained towels, tea towels, tablecloths and Nana's innumerable floral wrap around pinnies, standard dress for all valley wives.

It was the hair cutting equipment, however which attracted Alan and I one wet afternoon. Uncle Bill had given Granda a haircut the previous evening and we had watched, fascinated, as tufts of dark hair, sprinkled with grey had dropped onto the lino. The best part though were the clippers, which Bill ran up and down the back of Granda's neck. They, like the scissors, were silver, with two handles, which were squeezed to effect a very close cut, almost like a shave. After the haircut, uncle Bill had absent mindedly shoved the scissors and clippers into Nana's pinny drawer, instead of their rightful place on the top shelf.

Unnoticed, they lay there, until the following afternoon, when rain confined Alan and I to the kitchen. Nana was busy ironing, her metal flat irons heated on the fire, then pressed firmly over shirts, overalls and pinnies. The pinny drawer was open to receive the freshly ironed garments, and a glint of silver caught my eye. I lifted out the gleaming instruments all the more exiting because we were forbidden to touch them.

"Howay Alan" I whispered, "I'll give you a haircut"

Nana had her back to us, engrossed in her ironing. Alan was a willing victim and sat obediently on the crackett, while I set about his hair.

<u>**Alan, before the haircut, with Linda and I**</u>

The scissors were sharp and the ease with which handfuls of blonde hair fell to the floor was most satisfying. It was the clippers I really wanted to use though. Starting at the back of Alan's neck, as I'd seen uncle Bill do with Granda, I worked upwards. Somehow, I got carried away, and just kept on going, in no time, I had clipped a path right over the top of Alan's head, emerging at his forehead. Next, I started above his right ear and worked my way over to the left one. The end result was very eye catching, rather like a hot cross bun. Alan had four uneven clumps of hair sprouting, one on each quarter of his head. A punk rocker would have been proud of it!

"Right, I'll cut yours now" whispered Alan. We glanced at Nana, she was still busy, so we swapped places and I perched on the crackett, while Alan wielded the scissors. Soon, there was a goodly pile of my darker blonde hair mixed with Alan's platinum on the floor. Then I felt the tickle of the clippers as he started to run them across my head.

Doubt began to set in. I looked anxiously at the shorn heap. There seemed to be an awful lot of hair on the floor, and mine wasn't that long to start with. I capitulated.

"Nana, me hair's fallin' out"

"Oh aye" muttered Nana, still preoccupied with her work. "But me hair's fallin' out Nana" I repeated.

At last, she turned around. Her jaw dropped, and considering the sight, which met her eyes, it's no wonder!

We gazed back at her from beneath the remnants of our massacred hair. The iron sizzled its way gently through one of Granda's shirts as the seconds ticked by.

At last, she found her voice.
"Marcy me!" She breathed. "What ha' ye done?"
"We've cut wa hair," I answered.

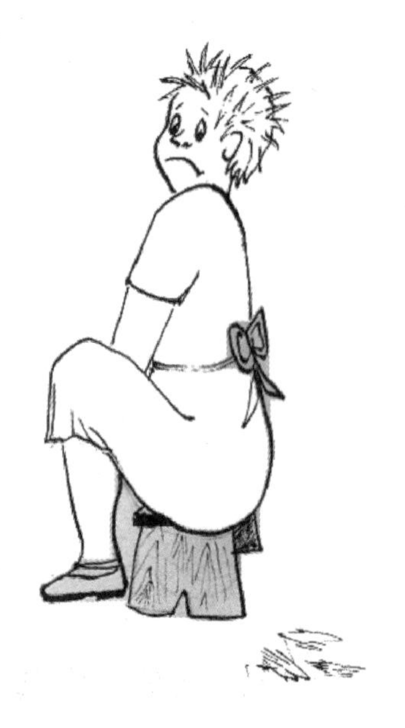

Cut yer hair! Marciful God! What'll yer mams' say when they see that lot? Ye look like a pair o' raggy mats! I dinna ken hoo wa ganna fettle this mess." She bustled into the scullery and returned bearing one of Granda's caps.

"Come here Alan. Clap this ower yer heed."

The cap was huge and made Alan look like a long stalked mushroom. I giggled, which proved to be a mistake. Nana rounded on me.

"And ye can wipe that smile off yer face, ye naughty lass. Bide there, while I find summat te cover yer heed."

Her eyes swept the room looking for something with which to hide my coiffeur. They stopped at the red knitted tea cosy. garnished with pom-pom, which covered the teapot.

"That'll dee." She said, and before I knew it, the tea cosy, still warm from its previous incumbent, was pulled down over my head, my ears sticking through the holes meant for handle and spout.

Every time I see a Rastafarian, I remember the ignominy of having to wear a tea cosy on my head. That, and the hilarity our appearance caused when Granda, Bill and Jim came home.

What a sight we must have been, two sheepish five year olds, resplendent in oversized cap and woolly tea cosy.

The men folk chuckled for days.

The Haircut

"What shall we play? It's a wet day
We can't go out in that
I'm fed up." Little Alan said, as gloomily he sat.
Nana ironed busily, her back towards us two
"Haad yer wheesht ye bairns and find something to do"
The cupboard door was open and inside, gleaming there
The scissors and the clippers Nana used on Granda's hair.
"Sit on the cracket Alan," I whispered in his ear
"I'll give you the best hair cut you've had in many a year"
The clippers made a close mown path across our Alan's pate
Then criss crossed over once again, he was a bonny state
Alan's head looked like a blondie hot cross bun
I snipped at the remaining hair, boy was I having fun!
"It's your turn now" said Alan as he vacated the seat
And wielded scissors with a will, as though clipping a sheep
I watched, dismayed, as tufts of hair passed floating to the floor
This seemed not such a good idea as it had seemed before
"Nana, my hair is falling out," I anxiously declared
The game no longer fun, as I was rapidly de-haired
"Oh aye?" our Nana muttered in a quite sarcastic tone.
"It really is man Nana nearly right down to the bone"
At last she turned and saw us, her expression was quite stunned
"Marcy me, you little tykes whatever have you done?"
"What will I tell your mammies when they see such a mess?"
The rest of what Nana said, I'll leave you all to guess
Our heads had to be covered up for some time after that
I remember I'd a woolly red tea cosy for a hat
Alan wore my Granda's cap, too big by a long shot
We had to wear them all the time, like the things or not
Eventually our hair grew back I'm very glad to say
But we never forgot the haircuts we got that rainy day.

Chapter Thirteen - Valley Folk.

I don't wish to give the impression that Alan and I were the only children up the valley. There were others, but the farms were so widely scattered that we hardly saw them, The Brodies at Blindburn had a son and two daughters, the elder of whom uncle Bill married in later years. There were twin boys on another farm, their father constantly exhorting all comers to -"Give them a bloody good hiding whenever you see them." On the grounds that, if they already hadn't been up to mischief, they soon would be.

The farthest flung farm was Uswayford. (Pronounced locally "Yoozyford') The family there boasted four children, at least two of whom still live in the valley today. The youngest girl, Mona, was about my age, so her father brought her with him once, when he came to discuss farm business with Granda. I suppose he thought it an ideal opportunity for two little girls to get together. Poor Mona, I don't know what she must have thought, but I was shy, and thoroughly intimidated by this dark haired girl, so I hid in the netty and wouldn't come out until she and her dad had gone. Mona's presence at Windyhaugh disturbed me. I was only a visitor to the valley, she really belonged. Much as I liked to think of myself as part of the local scene, Mona's presence reminded me that I was just an interloper. I hope she has forgiven my bad manners.

The school for the valley children was a single roomed stone building on the hillside above Barrowburn. Beside it, stood the schoolteacher's house, built of wood and painted grey and white. Behind both were some of the few trees then in upper Coquetdale. In front, was a view over Barrowburn and Windyhaugh as far as the point where river and valley take a turn to the left, heading for Carshope, Carlcroft, and Blindburn and beyond.

The schoolteacher then was Miss Trueman, a lady who seemed quite old to me, but then, anyone over thirty is old to a child, so perhaps she wasn't. At one stage, she had five of Aunty Peg's children in her school, which must have gone a long way towards justifying its existence, when the total pupil role was well under twenty.

On one occasion she was relating the story of "Noah's Ark." this was at a time when one particular farmer, whom we shall call 'Smith', farmed much of the valley, and his efforts to acquire more was the talk of the place.) Miss Trueman had reached the point in the story where Noah had released the dove, and it had returned, bearing an olive leaf.
"This meant that there was land showing somewhere children," she said. "So what do you think happened next?"
"Please Miss? called out Aunty Peg's Brian, "Smith bought it!"

It must have been a lonely life for Miss Trueman. living up there above the valley. Once in a while, her sister, Val, came to stay. An eccentric old lady, with white hair, which stood on end, quite unlike Miss Trueman's own neat dark locks.

One of her predecessors at the school had been a one armed schoolmaster, called Andrew Faa. He was reputed to have been a gypsy, educated by a land-owning lady on the Scottish side of the border, as compensation for the accident on her land in which he lost his arm.

Behind the schoolhouse began a track called "The Kylie Shin." A precipitous ledge which had an almost sheer drop of scree slope below it and seemed to me to be as narrow as a knife blade. It led to Fairhaugh and Uswayford. farms whose isolation made Windyhaugh seem as though it were in the middle of the A1.

The Brodies, Tom and Jessie, from Blindburn, had made their first home in the valley at Fairhaugh, so all their household effects had to be taken by horse and cart along the kylie shin. It was an extremely wild day, with wind howling through the hills.

Jessie stayed with the hospitable folk of Barrowburn. While Tom made the several trips needed to transport all their worldly goods to Fairhaugh. She was to travel with the last load, which also included their pig.

They had some difficulty persuading the pig to make the journey, when its turn came. But eventually, it was manhandled into the cart.

The horse, meanwhile, must have been just about at the end of its tether. After all, he had manfully (or horse-fully!) struggled back and forwards along a treacherous track in atrocious weather, pulling a heavily laden farm cart.

To be expected to haul a pig as well was more than flesh and blood could stand, so, in Jessie's words, " the horse reisted. " That is, he dug in his hooves and refused to move the cart one inch with the pig aboard.

There was nothing for it, the pig had to be evicted!

However, having been reluctant to board in the first place, she was damned if she was going to disembark.

Tom Brodie was one of nature's great gentlemen, but I think that even his patience must have worn a little thin before the disgruntled pig was finally persuaded out of the cart and tethered to the back.

The disgruntled pig

The horse was prepared to tolerate this arrangement, so Jessie climbed aboard and off they set on the final journey to their new home at Fairhaugh.

Jessie must have wondered what wild part of the world they were coming to, as the wind lashed her cheeks rosy and the cart lurched along the hair-raising track. However, she looked around with interest at her new surroundings, until her eye lit on a piece of furniture at the foot of the scree slope.

"Marcy me!" She called, "There's some poor body's settee doon ower the brae face."

Unfortunately, it turned out to be hers! Blindburn, when they moved there, must have seemed quite a metropolis, with its two attending cottages and a hard road to the place I don't suppose moving day was half as exciting though!

Moving Day

"Tom and Jessie Brodie are moving in today"
Liza said to Geordie, "D you think they will stay?
In such an isolated spot with no real road up to it
I hope they settle in all right and don't begin to rue it"

"They'll be alright Liza, in fact here they come now"
The wagon with their furniture, the horse and cart and cow
Liza warmly greeted the new young man and wife
Who were heading for their first home to begin a shepherds life

"There isn't any road up to your billet you young pair
You'll have to shuttle stuff up on the cart to get it there"
"That's fine," said Tom, "We'll manage, we'll unload the wagon here
The horse and cart will do it in a few trips never fear."

"Now Jessie, just you bide here till the men have done the shifting
We can't have a young lass like you doing all that heavy lifting
Jess stood with Liza, watching as the cart was loaded up
With chairs and pots and pans and bits of furniture and stuff.

"They'll have to go quite carefully along the hillside track,
It's called the Kylie Shin and it's a few miles there and back."
Jessie watched the first cartload set off along its way
And hoped that her new furniture would see it through the day

Two or three loads later and the horse was getting slow
But there was one most precious load that finally had to go
The couple's greatest assets were a pig and a house cow
The cow had gone up earlier, the pig was going now

But everyone forgot about the feelings of the horse
He'd hauled that cart up hill, down dale
through burns and even worse
The last and worst indignity was seeing that pig loaded
Never had a willing horse been so unfairly goaded

He flatly dug his hooves in and he just refused to shift
He'd carry anything at all, but a pig he wouldn't lift
Eventually calm returned, the pig was disembarked
"I'll tie her to the back and she can follow," Tom remarked

Jessie climbed on board between Tom and a hen meal bin
And off they trundled to their home along the Kylie Shin
Eagerly Jess looked around at the hills where they would settle
Its lonely beauty put her in a most contented fettle

And then she cried "Oh look down yonder over the brae face
There's some poor body's settee. What's it doing in that place?"
Tom hummed and hawed and harrumped while
he thought of a reply
Jessie's eyes grew wider as she realised just why

"D'you mean to tell me that's my new settee down there?
I told you when you set out with it to take extra care.
I thought it was a strange place for someone to leave a seat!
Aye well Tom, you can rest there when you go to look the sheep

Chapter Fourteen- The Country Polis

There was rarely any need for the local policeman to come up the valley on business, but like all good local bobbies, ours kept in touch with the people on his patch. Occasionally, therefore, red faced, puffing and sweating, on his bike, would come the local representative of the thin blue line, to call in on the valley folk.

Jock was always made welcome. It was no easy journey on a pushbike, and people appreciated that he had made the effort. They also enjoyed the different slant on life which he gave them. Nana would tut tut in disapproval of the roguish goings on of some of his customers, whilst pressing on him more tea and scones fresh from the girdle. Jock relayed his tales with great relish, basking in the admiration which was unstintingly given

"Aah wadna like te deal wi' the likes 'o' yon Jock." Nana would say, and he would go on to tell her and Granda of the crime wave, which, to hear him talk, was sweeping the apparently sleepy towns and villages in the county.

He wasn't above playing a practical joke or two on his flock either. We laughed till the tears ran down our faces at the trick Jock and his sidekick played on the patrons of a well known local pub. It was a snowy night and waiting in the freezing cold to supervise "Chuckin out time, " the pair of them hatched a plot. They got down on their knees, placing their boots in front of their kneecaps and spreading their police capes around them. On their departure from the pub, the inebriated customers were greeted by what looked like two of Snow White's dwarfs in police uniform.
"Howay oot 'o' there ye drunken divels. We've waited that lang in the wet, we've bloody well shrunk'."
According to Jock, some of them forswore the demon drink for as long as a week afterwards'.

Once, Jock called when Mam was at Windyhaugh, and as a policeman's wife herself, she was able to regale him with tales of life in the police force on the outskirts of Newcastle. The police house we lived in incorporated two cells, which were rarely used for the purpose for which they were intended, they were, however, bitterly cold. Jellies set beautifully in them. So, in the absence of a fridge, it was Mam's custom to leave the jellies and trifles for Sunday, in the cells on a Saturday night. A truculent drunk, spending one Saturday night as a guest of Her Majesty, emerged next day, beaming and replete, and we had tinned fruit and evaporated milk for our Sunday pudding!

Mam and Jock swapped stories for some time before they realised that they had a police acquaintance in common, a fellow with a wonderful way with words.

"De ye mind the time the press asked him about the river rising in the middle of Morpeth", asked Jock, and he told them, "The floods are debating."

"Yes and the time he told his men to, 'throw an accordion round the building!'" Laughed Mam.

"Grand detergent, them police dogs" Quoted Jock, and so it went on. Culminating in a story set in a local magistrates court one November.

The day was cold and wet. The court was packed with steaming people, waiting to see if the magistrate would grant extensions to their licensing hours, for various Christmas functions. The windowpanes ran with rain on the outside and condensation on the inside, but the proceedings were going like clockwork.

The rather officious clerk of the court read out the function, its venue, which organisation was holding it, and the date on which the extension was required. His rubber stamp was already descending on the permit, as the magistrate intoned, "Granted" after each request.

There were no objections to any of them, the pile of petitions was going down rapidly, and the proceedings were drawing towards a close, when the clerk read out, in his usual rapid monotone.

"Request by ——— Young Farmers Club, for an extension to the licence at The Black Bull Hotel on the evening of December 24th, for the purposes of a dinner dance."

His rubber stamp was already swooping down to endorse the expected permission, when our friend's considerable bulk rose to its feet.

"Howld on a minute." He paused for effect, as everyone stared at him in amazement. "Hev ye Thowt aboot this at all? This is an application by the Young Farmers. They're ganna hev a dinner dance, and nee doot a canny few drinks. Hev ye thowt aboot the date 'o' this application? They want their extension on the night of December 24th," He paused again at this point and the outrage in his voice became even more pronounced.

"That means, all these drunken young farmers is ganna be rowlin' oot onti the streets 'o' the toon orly next mornin'. Hev ye thowt aboot what date that'll be?" He had his audience spell bound now, as he continued.
"It'll be December the twenty fifth, and on behalf of Jesus Christ, whose borthday it is, I OBJECT!"

He sat down again; arms folded across his massive chest and surveyed the astonished clerk defiantly. Recovering his composure, the clerk raised his eyebrows inquiringly in the direction of the magistrate.

"Request denied" was the verdict. The young farmers had to make other arrangements, and the birthday of Jesus passed off without any unseemly drunkenness on the streets of the little town, at least for that year!

Chapter Fifteen - Clipping And Dipping

There were some special times when valley folk got together to help each other with tasks which needed more manpower than each isolated farm could provide. Such times were clipping, dipping, and haymaking.

The first two had to do with sheep; I suppose the third did too, since the hay was required for winter feed for sheep, as well as cattle.

At clippings and dippings, the sheep pens really came into play. Having stood empty for much of the time, they were a hive of activity at these landmarks in the shepherd's year.

Clipping required dry weather, wet fleeces are no good. So at the appropriate season, as soon as we had a few dry days in a row, Granda, Bill and Jim, ably assisted by Tip, Bett and Sheddles, would start gathering the sheep from the surrounding hills. Dispersed about the hills, the sheep did not look many in number, but concentrated in one place, the world seemed to be full of them, and I was glad that they were timid, rather silly creatures, but harmless. The only time a ewe (pronounced "yow" hereabouts) ever shows aggressive tendencies, is when her lambs are threatened. Then she will stand her ground, albeit nervously, stamping her foot to warn off the intruder. Should you be unkind enough to persist in your harassment, she will usually turn tail and, making sure her lamb is with her, run off.

The nature of sheep is not aggressive, but when it comes to awkwardness, they can show us a thing or two. Granda, Bill and Jim would be sweating and swearing by the time they had them gathered in. Shouts and whistles to the dogs would reverberate round the hills, mingling with the frantic bleating of the sheep, who objected strongly to having their freedom curtailed

In the confusion, ewes and lambs would be separated, and they were more intent on finding each other than in going in the required direction. Eventually, however, they would all be shepherded into an 'in by' field, ready for the clipping to begin. Alan and I must have been proper nuisances, darting about and getting in the way, but the excitement and urgency of the occasion infected us. Granda gave us our own cut down horn headed sticks so that we could "help", but I have no doubt that things would have proceeded much more smoothly without us There was many a cry of

"Hout! Git oot the road, ye little divels!"

On the day appointed for clipping to begin, Geordie Murray and Tom (his surname, I discovered years later, was Hall, but he was always known as "Tom 'o' Barrowburn") would turn up to help, with their attending sheepdogs, and wielding their clippers. Not the electric shavers used nowadays. These were metal scissors with a stiff spring, which required strong hands and wrists to use them.

A flock of ewes, and unavoidably, their lambs, were persuaded by the dogs into the main area of the sheep pens. One of the men would plunge in among them and haul out a wide-eyed ewe, then another, and another, until all the clippers were supplied with victims. Using the horns as handles, the men would tip the sheep up until they were sitting on their rumps in a most ungainly position, looking absolutely ludicrous.

They looked even more ludicrous when divested of their coats, like plucked turkeys, or men in their long Johns. The half grown lambs were excused this indignity, and released back into the holding field to be reunited with their half naked mothers. The fleeces were swiftly and expertly rolled up and thrown onto a large sheet of hessian, which would later be wrapped around them for their journey out of the valley.

The lanolin in fleeces is the basic ingredient of most hand creams; So Granda and the others had hands which would have done credit to any, lady after clipping time.

Diverting as it was to watch the antics of sheep and shepherds, Alan and I began to feel that we were superfluous to requirements, and that would never do!
"Come ower here a minute" Alan whispered, "De ye fancy a go at clipping?" He asked.
"Diven't be see daft" I said scornfully, "They'll never let us at the sheep"
"Hadaway woman! I wasn't meaning THOR sheep." He said, glancing disdainfully at the sheep pens.
"Well which ones do you mean?"
"What aboot the pet lambs, we could clip them."

There were three half grown pet lambs in the small field past the pigsty, so we set off in their direction.
"What are we ganna clip them with though Alan? We canna pluck them like hens!" I asked in dismay.
"Dinna worry, aah've got me Granda's owld clippers under me ganzy.
" Sure enough, from under his jumper, Alan produced a pair of rather old, but still serviceable sheep shears. He tried them out on a tuft of grass, but to our consternation, neither of us had the strength in our hands to force them shut.

Permanently open shears were as much use as a three wheeled tractor, so some other plan would have to be concocted
"What aboot me Nana's kitchen scissors." I suggested. "You know, the ones she uses to cut the strings on the sacks of meal."
"Aye, they'll dee fine," said Alan, cheering up as he realised we were back on course "Hadaway and seek them then."
I strolled into the scullery with as innocent an air as I could muster.

Nana was bustling about getting dinner ready for all hands, so she didn't notice me remove the scissors and skip out again. Once, out of the door, I ran, scattering hens and ducks, round the corner of Sally's sty, to where Alan was eyeing up the pet lambs.
"Which yin forst?" He asked.

The lambs were falling over themselves in their eagerness to be "forst. " The poor things assumed that we had brought their feeds, so it wasn't a question of catching them, more a question of beating them back. They were named after comic strip characters of the time, Pip, Squeak, and Wilfred, and it was poor old Squeak who drew the short straw simply because he had pushed his way to the front. Alan grabbed him by the neck and hung on. At this point, it began to dawn on Squeak that feeding him was not what we had in mind, and he began to struggle.

"Howay man! Help us to coup him ower. " Gasped Alan, red in the face. I grabbed Squeak's back legs, and at some risk to myself, pulled them towards me. Squeak obligingly couped over backwards, but so did Alan, with Squeak on top of him.

"Oomph!" The wind was knocked out of Alan, but with commendable determination, he hung on, and with my help, managed to manoeuvre himself into more or less the classic clipping position. Squeak, sitting on his rump, looked astonished at this turn in events, but for some reason, when sheep are sat on their rear ends, they give up the struggle, so he more or less acquiesced in what followed.

"Hoy us the scissors, " panted Alan.
"Its dangerous to hoy scissors, " I argued.
"Aah ken that fine woman!" Alan was showing signs of temper. "Just give them here." I passed him the scissors, but he couldn't both hold onto Squeak and wield the scissors.
"Ye'll hetta dee it yersel" he said "Gan on, start at his heed."

There wasn't much wool on Squeak's head, so I ignored Alan's advice, and began to clip along his side, snipping dainty little clumps of wool here and there. I repeated this operation on his other side. By this time Alan was exhausted.
"I'll hetta let gan. Stand back."

Squeak pounded away and gave a little skip of relief. We turned to survey the fleece. It was very disappointing. Granda and the other experts produced a whole fleece, as though the sheep had taken off a coat. All we had was a little pile of loose wool, like the bits that get snagged on barbed wire fences. We looked at Squeak, who still hung around hoping for a feed. Somehow. he didn't look at all like the ewes newly released from clipping. Re looked more like a moth eaten raggy mat

There was a long silence while we considered the results of our labours.

"Aye well, mebese we'll make a better job of the next yin," said Alan doubtfully. You can keep a hadden it and aah'll dee the clippin'. " He announced, confidence returning. Keeping hold of it was easier said than done. Pip and Wilfred were still nuzzling round us as pet lambs do, so Pip was selected, on the grounds that she was the smallest, therefore easier for me to hold. I grabbed her round the neck from behind, and with Alan's help, got her onto her rump. More by good luck than good judgement, I ended up with my back against the wall; otherwise even Pip's small weight would have knocked me over backwards. I hung on grimly, while Alan, scissors in hand, set to.

Like me, he began with the flanks, but he was much more organised in his approach, clipping under the fleece in straight lines until he had lifted a flap of wool on one side. He gave her other side the same treatment, and then the problem was how to make the two areas meet.

The part of her anatomy he needed to reach. right down her spine, was firmly wedged against my legs.

"Can ye no torn her roond a bit?" he demanded.

"Torn her roond yerself! " I shouted, worn out with the effort of hanging onto Pip, and very uncomfortable squashed against the wall. I must have relaxed my grip for an instant. because, with a wriggle, Pip was free and running across the field, her two loose side panels of wool flapping like wings. If she'd been a horse, she'd have looked like Pegasus. Her appearance was so comical, that Alan soon got over his disappointment at not completing the job.

We looked at each other for a moment and dissolved into fit of giggles. Soon, we were rolling about consumed with laughter, the kind that wont stop.

We were still laughing when Nana came looking for us for our dinner. "Hout, yee bairns! Did ye no hear me shootin' on ye te come for yer dinner? Howay in and eat it while its hot. What are ye laughin' at anyway?"

"Helpless with merriment, I pointed at Pip and Squeak. Pip had stopped running, so she looked quite normal, her flaps hanging close to her side, but there was no disguising Squeak's moth eaten appearance.

"Marciful heaven! Ha' ye been ploatin' the poor beast? Jack! Jack! Come here," she shouted. Granda rounded the corner, followed by uncle Bill, Geordie, Tom 'o' Barrowburn and all their dogs.
"Just look ower yonder." Said Nana, pointing at Squeak. "Thor bairns has been howkin' lumps oot 'o' the poor lamb!
"No we haven't Nana," Alan spoke up, "We've been clippin' like me Granda"
"Clippin'! Aah'll clip yer lugs, ye little divels" said Granda, but he was smiling, so we knew he didn't mean it. The sudden appearance of so many people and dogs, however, had alarmed the lambs and made them run towards the far corner of the field.

"Jack, I think ye better weigh yon lamb doon afore she takes off" rumbled Geordie, poker faced
"Aye, either that, or get her a pilot's licence" added Tom
Pip on the run was a strange sight, like a woolly aeroplane heading up the runway ready for take off.

Uncle Bill was the first to give in. With a spluttered, "Well I go te hell! He was convulsed with laughter. Granda, Geordie and Nana were next. Even Tom, ever poker faced, permitted himself a smile. So ended my first and last attempt to clip a sheep.

I felt a little sorry for the sheep being clipped, although I'm sure they felt better for it afterwards, but I felt Heartily sorry for them at dipping time. Doubtless it was for their own good and rid them of many harmful parasites, but they weren't to know that.

As at clipping time, the sheep were gathered into a holding field, then batches of them were herded into the holding pens. This time, there was no escape for the lambs, they, almost as big as their mothers by now, had to undergo trial by sheep dip too. The sheep bath was filled with yellow, strong smelling dip, and no sheep in its right mind would venture into it voluntarily.

This natural reticence was catered for - Granda would grab them by the back of the neck and the rump and drop them over the edge into the bath.

They could all swim of course, but the rules declare that they must be submerged in dip, so uncle Bill or Jim or Geordie Murray, would stand astride the sheep bath and push them under with shepherds crooks.

The poor beasts would bob up again and scramble up the ramp at the other side, dyed bright yellow and frantic to get as far from the sheep bath as they could.

Chapter Sixteen - Haymaking.

Haymaking time was the season I liked best of all.

It involved the women and children, as well as the men, in fact, they made up an important part of the work force.

Haymaking began with Granda, Bill and Jim cutting the hay with scythes.

I once tried cutting thistles with a scythe. Even with Granda guiding my hand, I couldn't do it. It is a task, which requires skill and rhythm, so I was full of admiration for the seemingly effortless way the men cut the crop of hay.

While they were engaged in this task, they didn't even come back to the house for meals. Nana would make sandwiches, wrapped in red "bait hankies" and produce a billy can full of tea, then I would bear them proudly to the hay field, where I was greeted warmly, as much as a herald of the bait time break as for myself.

I usually took my own bait too, and the four of us sat chomping on our sandwiches in the dyke back.

There is no pleasanter smell than that of newly cut hay - I can't imagine why some perfume or after-shave manufacturer has not bottled it.

I'm sure they would make a fortune if they could capture that aroma of summer sunshine.

Linda and I in the hayfield with Uncle Jim on the Pike

I suppose present day haymakers have radios in the enclosed cabs of their tractors and count themselves lucky. Little do they know what they are missing, we were serenaded by skylarks soaring overhead, with the occasional curlew calling from the hills, the river gurgling a background to it all.

The hay was left lying in the sun until the exposed side was dry, when it had to be turned over for the sun to dry the other side. Granda constantly scanned the sky for rain clouds at this time, because, if it rained, the drying out process would have to begin all over again. Too many soakings, and the hay, vital for winter feed, was ruined.

On the day that it was finally deemed ready to be brought in, the hay field buzzed with activity. Nana, Liza and Mary from Barrowburn and usually, Aunty Peg, all in colourful floral aprons would join the men. Even families from other farmsteads up the valley would appear, the women and children wielding wooden hay rakes, the men clutching two-pronged hayforks.

Everyone brought their bait with them, so all along the dyke backs there were little clutches of bright bait hankies and billycans of tea, waiting for the meal break.

We all set to work with a will, laughing and chattering with our neighbours. The women making full use of this opportunity for a good gossip, but never pausing, as they raked the hay into long rows up and down the field. Next it was raked into little piles at regular intervals, then the men would start building it into the mini haystacks called 'pikes'. As soon as a few pikes were built, Granda and Geordie would seek the hay bogies - low flat carts onto which the pikes were loaded for the journey back to the stackyard. This was the part we children loved. We would wait until the pike was winched aboard, then dump our hay rakes and jump onto the bogie, our backs against the hay and our feet dangling over the edge.

We would sing at the tops of our voices all the way back to the stackyard, competing for volume with the roar of the tractor, or, if the bogie were horse drawn, fitting the rhythm of our song to the clop of Dick's hooves.

In the stackyard, more of the valley men would be waiting to unload the pikes and fork them into the hayshed. In a good year, it would be filled almost to the roof, and a haystack thatched with straw would be built in the stackyard. The house martins. who made their homes in the hayshed, didn't seem in the least put out by this activity. They swooped in and out as usual, skimming within inches of us at times, though another resident of the hayshed made her disapproval quite plain.

Nana had acquired a couple of Muscovy ducks, exotic looking creatures who couldn't quack and liked to roost on a high perch. I didn't class them as real ducks at all, much preferring the busy little Khaki Campbells.

Uncle Bill was beavering away lifting forkfuls of hay onto the pile in the hayshed, when one of the muscovies, perched up on a beam, decided to relieve herself. The squashy mess went right down the back of uncle Bill's neck!

"Hout! Ye dorty shitten little bugger!" Yelled Bill, aiming his hayfork, spear - like in the direction of the offending duck. It fell far short of the mark, and the duck, unabashed, fixed him with its unblinking eye and began preening its feathers.

"Just wait till aah get ahadden ye! Aah'll ploat every feather off yer backside, ye dorty article!"

The bogie load of children, who had arrived in time to see it all, danced about with delighted laughter, until uncle Bill stripped off his ruined shirt and began swiping it playfully at us.

Aah'll teach ye te laugh at me, ye little divels, aah'll plaster ye wi this lot and see hoo ye like it!"

Geordie Murray, watching this pantomime with a twinkle in his eye, drawled,

"Aye well Bill, it could ha been worse. It could ha been a coo up yonder!

"It couldn't ha dropped a bigger load if it had been a bloody cow," said Bill, grinning ruefully and vanishing into the house for a wash and a clean shirt.

For a few days the work continued, and hayfields and stackyard were alive with happy activity. Then, the workforce moved on to the next farm whose hay was ready to be gathered in.

Hay making at Windyhaugh.

The women all have gathered
In the hayfield by the hill
They chatter as they ply
Their wooden hay rakes with a will

Their brightly patterned aprons
Light up the field like flowers
Their laughter on the summer breeze
Gladden the working hours

The men wielding their pitch forks
Are stacking up the hay
Each load, a blessing harvested
Against a winters day

The Skylarks swoop and warble
And pierce the sky with song
The river sings a counterpoint
Its timeless path along

Glistening in the dyke back
Beside the dry stone wall
The billy cans and bait boxes
With food enough for all

The children run with laughter
And clamber on the cart
Those golden days will stay
Forever etched upon my heart

Chapter Seventeen - The Stack yard.

The stack yard, even when not the hive of activity which it was at haytime, was still a fascinating place for a child. A frequent resident was the wooden cart (pronounced keeart) which Dick, the carthorse pulled. When not in use it normally stayed, aptly enough, in the cart shed, but if it was going to be used again fairly quickly, it was often left in the stackyard, resting on its shafts.

At the end of one happy day in the hayfield, I hopped down from the last trip on the bogie, and noticed the fine slope presented by the resting cart.
"Hey, Alan, look at the cart. Wouldn't that make a grand slide?" "Bye, yer right, it would that!" Alan enthused. "I'm having first go, it was my idea." I stated. "Right you are, but we'd better wait until they all clear off then we can have as many goes as we like." said the wily Alan.

We dawdled about the stackyard until the bogie had been unhitched, parked for the night and Granda and the others had gone back to the house. As soon as they'd vanished. I hoisted myself up onto the high end of the cart. I tucked my frock into my knickers, so that it wouldn't get dirty, and sat down ready to enjoy the swoop down the slope. Then I let go.

What followed imprinted itself on my memory, as well as on my behind. The grain of the wood was facing up the slope! So that by the time I reached the bottom, my backside looked like a hedgehog, and I was whimpering with pain. Alan, seeing that all was not well, ran to fetch Nana. She came, followed by Aunty Peg and the men. Their concern soon gave way to laughter, Aunty Peg especially, was almost hysterical. The only one who treated the situation with the seriousness I felt it deserved was Nana. With a "Marcy me! The poor bairn!" She swept me up and carried me into the house. The others staggered along behind, rocking with laughter. The supper was quickly cleared from the table, and replaced by me, bottom up. I could hear Alan, Bill, Jim and Granda howling with merriment in the scullery, while Nana and Aunty Peg set to with the tweezers, extracting splinters.

It must be said, that Peg wasn't much help. Her hands were shaking too much, but she did her best, between wiping the tears of laughter from her eyes. After what seemed like a very long time, the last splinter was removed, my poor behind was bathed with a solution of bicarb and water, then rubbed with salve, the ointment for all eventualities, kept in the kitchen press.

Ministrations over, Nana cuddled me in to her enormous, comforting bosom and let me cry my fill. The others had managed to straighten their faces by this time, and clucked around me sympathetically. I ate my supper standing up that night, and slept on my stomach. Even the feather mattress was too much for my sore bottom to bear!

The stackyard was also the home of a strange machine, which looked like a cross between a steam organ and a covered wagon minus the cover. To complete the ridiculous picture, the whole thing was painted bright pink!

This was the thresher. Usually when I was at Windyhaugh, it squatted, unused, in the stackyard, looking rather like a fat lady in a pink frock. I was, however, privileged to see it in action once. It was on a short visit one autumn, when the oats were being threshed. I heard a dreadful noise coming from the stackyard, and ran round to investigate.

The sight, which met my eyes, was incredible. The normally stolid thresher was attached by means of a canvas belt, to the drive wheel of the tractor. Both tractor and thresher were making a tremendous din, and the thresher was jiggling about like a jelly. The fat lady in the pink frock was doing the shimmy!

The tractor was her hen-pecked dancing partner, and the unexpected sight reduced me to a fit of uncontrollable giggles. Dancing attendance on the two machines was a group of busy men. Geordie was hurling sheaves of oats up to Granda. who, with uncle Jim, was perched on top of the thresher. Granda caught each one and deftly cut the binding string before passing it to uncle Jim, who fed it bit by bit into the thresher's mouth. On the ground, uncle Bill was beside its spout, from which the threshed oats hurtled into sacks. It was his role to remove each sack as it filled.

The air was full of dust and the noise of the machines. The stack of sheaves was getting lower, so their task would soon be completed. Just then, from the corner of my eye. I noticed a different kind of movement near the remains of the stack of sheaves. It was a grey tide, which, when I looked harder through the dust, sorted itself out into individual rats and mice. dozens of them! In a flash, I understood why the men had strings tied tightly round their trouser legs - the rats and mice were looking for any available bolthole, and they weren't too choosy!

I climbed up onto the bogie to get out of their way.

Uncle Bill, meanwhile, seemed to have decided to join the thresher and tractor in their dance. He was leaping about like a six-foot leprechaun, clutching one leg and yelling at the top of his voice. The other men downed tools and watched this performance with interest.
"Bloody hell!" he bellowed, "There's a rat up me troozer leg!"
"Ye'd best keep a hadden it then lad." Drawled Geordie
"Keep a hadden it! Aah'il strangle the little perisher, somebody come and help me then'." Shouted Bill. None of them made a move, all watching with interest to see how Bill would deal with this emergency.

"Howay man!" yelled Bill, a note of desperation in his voice. Eventually, Granda clambered down and strolled over. taking care to avoid the thinning stream of rodents, and the farm cats who were after them.
"I'll keep a hadden yer leg higher up so it canna get past. You see if ye can force it back doon.
Granda clasped Bill's leg in an iron grip
"OW!" he yelled "Yer ganna squeeze me bloody leg off! Yer worse than the rat!
"Aye well, " said Granda, "At least aah havna got designs on yer valuables. This'll teach ye te tie yer nicky tams a bit tighter. Howay noo, get crackin' and shift the damned thing."

I saw uncle Bill's hand working away below his knee, and then Granda reach out and grasp something protruding from below the trouser leg. He gave a swift pull and out came a large rat. It was in no fit state to care about its position however. It was as dead as a doornail and couldn't have been any flatter if a steamroller had gone over it!

Entertainment over, the men returned to complete their work.

The Slide (Notice how I put the blame on Alan)

I had a cousin, Alan
Who was full of good ideas
Although some of his boyish larks
Would finish up in tears

Like one time that he said to me
"I've found the grandest slide.
Instead of sitting at your books
Howay and play outside"

Through the farmyard Alan ran
With me right at his back
Into a stack yard where a cart
Was resting on its shafts

The slope that it presented
Was a prospect most inviting
The thought of sliding down it
Really was quite exciting

"Ladies first," my cousin said
In a manner most polite
(That really should have warned me
That something wasn't right)

I climbed up to the highest end
Of Granda's ancient cart
And hitched my frock into my nicks
All ready for the start

Off I went, straight down the slope
But oh, the shock! The pain!
That's one slide that I knew at once
I'd never use again

The grain of wood on that old cart
Was facing the wrong way
And quite a lot of it was now
Stuck in my bum to stay!

My bum looked like a hedgehog
With splinters sticking out
My Nana and my aunty Peg
Came running at my shout

"What on earths the matter
With the bairn," my Nana cried
I turned around and bent over
And showed them my backside

I didn't get the sympathy
That such a plight deserves
In fact, they couldn't help me
They were so consumed with mirth

I was taken to the kitchen
Laid face down upon the table
Nana and Peg pulled out the spelks
As fast as they were able

Their tears of laughter fell upon
My poor besplintered rear
My outraged yells reverberated
Round for all to hear

That evening at our suppertime
We gathered round to eat
But I consumed my supper
Firmly standing on my feet.

Chapter Eighteen - Evening Tales

If the days were never short of entertainment, the evenings could have been. After all, we had no television or radio, in fact, we didn't even have electricity! This may sound deadly dull, but it wasn't. When it began to darken, the oil lamps were lit to give a soft and friendly light, and we settled down around the fire with several options open to us.

One of them was the wind up gramophone, which lay resplendent in its own highly polished cabinet. The lid lifted up on top to reveal the turntable, with its horn and the kind of playing arm which required a new needle for every other record. Underneath was a cupboard which housed the record collection. These were mainly Scottish dance music, Jimmy Shand and his band being particular favourites.

The contraption had to be wound up first, by means of a handle on the side, and if it hadn't been sufficiently wound, the whole thing slowed down so that even Jimmy Shand's band took on a mournful tone. on the other hand, if you kept on winding, you could make poor Jimmy play at a furious pace until he sounded quite comical.

There were books to read in companionable silence, while Granda worked away carving his latest stick, Teaser, his border terrier at his feet. Card games were a favourite pastime too, but the happiest evenings were spent just talking. I especially loved to hear uncles Bill and Jim relay tales of their school days

They had a long walk to school through the border countryside in the company of their older brother, (my father) and another boy of similar age. Someone along their route kept goats, including a billy goat, which was kept tethered.

It was the daily habit of this other boy to tease the poor creature as he passed. His aim being, to make it charge him, knowing full well that the rope would run out long before it reached him, and the billy goat would be brought to a sudden jarring halt.

The three brothers stood this for so long, then they decided that it was high time the odds were shortened in favour of the goat.

One morning, they set off early, and lengthened its rope. They waited for the goat tormentor to appear, then sat back to watch the pantomime.

True to form, he started dancing around the goat, just outside the limits of its usual tether. Not content with that, he threw clods of grass and earth at it until it was thoroughly annoyed. He completed the performance in his usual way, by dropping his trousers and exposing his buttocks just outside the goat's reach.—— or so he thought'.

Billy's revenge was swift and merciless. The newly lengthened rope enabled him to but the tantalising buttocks fair and square, and knock his persecutor clear into the next field.

"Aye, I mind he was off school for a week." concluded uncle Bill with satisfaction.

Another tale I never tired of was one uncle Bill told of a small country school he attended with his brothers and sister. It was presided over by a veritable dragon. Who took pleasure in denying the younger children access to the toilet until it was too late, and then walloping them for their lack of control. She also hogged the fireside, which heated their one roomed school in winter, and left the children to shiver.

Bill and his brothers must have been the heroes of the school for the revenge they took on her.

She had her own private toilet. A shed of corrugated iron sheets bolted together, which stood in splendid isolation at one end of the school field.

She always entered this with an air of great superiority, slamming the door behind her, which must have been galling for the wet knickered pupils to whom she had denied this most basic facility.

One morning, uncle Bill and his brothers loosened almost every bolt in the structure, so that it was left standing with as much stability as a house of cards.

Morning break time arrived, and the children waited with baited breath for "Miss" to make her habitual visit. As usual, she entered with the air of a queen entering her throne room, slamming the door behind her. The building shuddered alarmingly, but the few remaining bolts were enough to hold it together.

Wriggling along the ground like red Indians, the brothers crept up, loosened the last bolts, and ran back to join the audience.

The walls of the shed quivered for a while, like the lips of her pupils so often reduced to distress. Then, almost triumphantly, they fell outwards, exposing the tyrant seated on her throne in all her glory.

Children can be merciless creatures, and they shrieked with laughter, dancing about and pointing at the horrified and humiliated woman.

She never did exercise the same control over them again. How could they possibly fear anyone who had been exposed to such ridicule.

"It wasna owwer lang eftor that that the owld bat left and we got a kinda half decent teacher" concluded uncle Bill.

Some evenings, we reminisced about visitors who had made the long journey to Windyhaugh - Mr Singleton, the tailor from Gosforth, who did so on a regular basis, to measure Granda, Bill or Jim for a new suit, or tried to sell Nana a new frock. Or the "one off" visitor, like "our Ann"

Ann was a relative of mine from my mother's side of the family, brought up in South Shields. Thinking that they were doing this city child a kindness Nana and Granda invited her to stay on the farm for a few days of fresh valley air.

All went well until Ann got her eye on Granda milking the cow, whereupon she was inconsolable.

"I don't like cow's milk, I just like horses milk" she wept. Naturally enough, everyone was very puzzled by this, until my mother explained that milk in South Shields was delivered by a horse and cart!

Those evenings round the fire in the lamplight were cosy, companionable affairs. Between anecdotes, Granda, Bill and Jim would discuss their day on the farm in their slow, Northumbrian drawl, all of which I found fascinating.

I liked it even better when one of the other valley men called in to while away the evening. If I sat very quietly on my little green crackett, they would forget I was there, and their conversation ranged more freely.

There were some wonderful characters among the hill farmers and shepherds in those days, including one Jim Armstrong, a shepherd in the College valley on the other side of Cheviot, who was the father of seventeen children. I spent a happy evening one summer, listening as Granda and Geordie Murray mused admiringly over some of his exploits.

"De ye mind the time the new vicar and hi wife moved into Kirknewton?"
"Aye" drawled Geordie, "and the poor sowls had nee bairns te their name."
"And soon eftor they moved in, Jimmy fetched a whole cartload of his bairns te be christened" Granda continued.
"Aye, Jimmy always waited till he had a cart-load and had them done in a job lot - kinda like a sheep dippin'"
At this point in the story, Granda took up the tale, affecting a genteel English accent
"My word, Mr Jackson" says the vicar, "What a fine family of children you have there. It must be the good fresh air in the hills. Unfortunately, my own dear wife has no children."
"De ye say so'" says Jimmy, "well, why don't you fetch her up for a visit"
"That is most kind of you Mr Jackson, I'll do that."

Geordie and Granda smiled to themselves as they recalled the next part of the story. Apparently, one day the vicar and his wife set off in their pony and trap, arriving at the Jackson's isolated cottage, just as he was coming in from a day's work on the hills. Granda recounted Jim's words.
"I see you've browt her then. I'm just doon from the hill, but if ye can hang on till I've had a cup of tea and a scone. I'll fettle her for ye."

At that, Granda, Geordie, Bill and Jim roared with laughter. I didn't really understand why, but something told me that if I drew attention to myself by asking, there would be no more stories to listen to that night, so I kept quiet.

Another tale I heard, the humour of which escaped me at the time, concerned an old friend of my Nana's family. A colourful character and a keen fisherman, he had been trying his hand with the fishing rod just outside the village, when a lady approached him. She was of a religious turn of mind, and sensing a possible convert, sat down beside him, proclaiming.

"Ah, Mr. Bell, you may be fishing for fishes, but I am fishing for men!"

Without a break in his concentration, he replied. "Ye'll no catch many hinny. Yer Sittin' on yer bait'."

This character was the subject of many an amusing evening conversation.

Another story concerned his efforts to join up at the outbreak of war. He had a rather unfortunate disfigurement, in that the Good Lord had seen fit to place his mouth round to one side of his face, rather than the more usual centre front position.
This bothered him not a jot, but caused some consternation to the examining officer when he went for his army medical, to sign up for World War II.

"I'm terribly sorry Mr. Bell, but I'm afraid we cannot pass you fit for the army." He explained.

"Why the hell not?" Exploded the perfectly fit Tommy Bell.

Trying to be tactful, the officer explained that it was his unusually placed mouth which was the problem.

"Huh!" said Tommy, 'Aah thowt ye wanted me te shoot Garmans, not worry the buggers!" and stalked out.

Granda and the others roared with laughter, even though I didn't always understand them, I loved their tales, and their obvious pleasure in recounting them.

When I did eventually climb the stairs to my feather bed, my way was lit by a candle set in a holder like the ones often seen in illustrations of "Wee Willie Winkie. " A stone hot water bottle warmed my feet, and the sound of the Coquet lulled me to sleep.

The Travelling Tailor

Every now and then along the Coquet Valley road
Came a little van, a gentleman and his extra special
load
A very welcome caller, a tailor of repute,
Mr Singleton of Gosforth, came to measure for a suit.
My granda would submit with grace to ordeal by tape measure.
While swatches of material were presented for his pleasure.
The choosing of the cloth was done with great deliberation,
The resultant garment would be for an auspicious occasion.
The measurements were written down, the style that he would make,
And then the main event, the tea and gossip and the cake.
Mr Singleton brought news from up and down the Cheviot Hills,
From exotic climes like Gosforth, from mansions, farms and mills,
And then before he left, a parting gift he would bestow
A floral wrap round pinny which left Nana's face aglow.
The family would gather round to wave him on his way,
And off he'd go to his next call to brighten up their day.

Chapter Nineteen - Trips to Alwinton.

The nearest pub to Windyhaugh was the Rose and Thistle at Alwinton, about six miles away, so, due to lack of transport, visits to it were not very frequent.

Occasionally though, uncle Bill would walk the two or three miles down the valley to a farm where they actually owned a car!

There, he could hitch a lift to the pub to enjoy a pint or two in the friendly company of the regulars, and Mr. Forman, the publican.

I expect Bill's lift was glad of his company on the return journey. Their house was at the other side of the river, and though there was a footbridge and a ford, the car was far too precious to leave on the other side of the river, or drive through the ford.

Therefor the father of the household and his three stalwart sons would take a corner each, and lift the car bodily over the burn to park it safely beside the house. When Bill was there, he took a corner, releasing the father to the role of overseer.

Uncle Bill then had a long walk home with wet feet. The farm gate was always left open for him on these nights, but once, Granda forgot and closed the gate.

Next morning Bill was sporting a very bruised and swollen nose.

What happened te yer nose uncle Bill?" I asked, "Did somebody at the pub hit you?"

"Nowt the kind" answered Bill, rather shortly, "I was hit by a gate."
"How did that happen?" I asked doubtfully, suspecting another of uncle Bill's jokes

"Well, it was as black as the earl 'o' hell's waistcoat last night,soI had a hand held out in front of me to feel the way. Well, me airm must have gone between the bars of the gate,'cause the next thing I knew,me nose was stotted off the top bar."

He smiled ruefully and rubbed his damaged nose gently. "It'stheforsttime I knew me nose waslangerthanme airm!"

Tom'o' Barrowburn's visits to the pub were even rarerthan Bill's-once a year on Alwinton Showday. AlwintonShow has alwaysbeenthe premier agricultural show for hill meninthe area. It is primarily a hill shepherd's show and none of the valley men would ever contemplate missingit. Even Tom o' Barrowburn made the journey down the valley to enjoy a day at the show and an evening at the Rose and Thistle afterwards.

After one such Alwinton show, Tom was offered a lift home on the pillion of a motor-bike, the proud acquisition of young Dode Brodie of Blindburn.

Tom never went anywhere without his stick, it was like an extension to his right arm, so when he climbed onto the motor bike, he was of course, clutching his stick. He rammed his cap down firmly onto his head, clenched his teeth, and off they went. It must have been a hair-raising journey for Tom, who'd never travelled on anything faster than an ancient tractor, but it went quite well, until they came to the first corner. As the motorbike leaned over to take the bend, Tom, thinking it was falling over, clamped his stick down onto the road.

The effect was dramatic. Tom and Dode were catapulted into the dykeback, followed by the motorbike. They could have been badly injured, but Tom's greatest concern was that he'd snapped his best stick!

Tom's Stick.

Old Tom had walked to Alwinton
To have a pint or two
He'd looked the sheep and milked the cow
So nowt else left to do

Young Dode was home a visiting
On shore leave from his ship
And everyone enjoyed the tales
About his latest trip

The hour was late so old Tom
Took his crook up in his hand
Said his good nights to one and all
And creaked upright to stand

"You're never walking home tonight
old Tom!" said sailor Dode
"Just wait until I've sunk this pint
I'll take you down the road."

Outside, beside a dry stone wall
The source of young Dode's pride
A gleaming motorbike on which
He offered Tom a ride

Tom settled his cap on his head
Hefted his trusty stick
Grabbed tight a hold round Dodie's waist
(He'd heard these bikes went quick)

Away they went up Coquetdale
Which is a winding road
Tom never had gone such a speed
And kept tight hold of Dode

One of the bends was pretty sharp
The bike leaned down to take it
But Tom, unused to such a slant
Thought they weren't going to make it

His trusty stick, his 'extra leg'
Plonked down to save his fall
Catapulted both of them
Right over Geordie's wall

"What happened there?" young Dodie cried
"My bike went out from under"
"Oh hell" said Tom "Just look at yon
My best sticks smashed asunder"

"Oh blast your stick, see my new bike
It's lying in the Coquet
Next time you have your stick with you
Just watch out where you poke it"

The bike retrieved, young Dodie said
"Next time Tom, you can hike
And please remember you can't
Pole vault on a motor bike!"

Chapter Twenty – Great Aunt Janet.

One year when I arrived for my usual summer stay, I found another resident installed at Windyhaugh. She was great aunt Janet, Granda's widowed half sister.

Great Aunt Janet's Passport Photograph.

She had decided, at her advanced age, to emigrate to Australia to join her son, however, Australia did not meet with her stringent requirements, so, two years later, back she came, and was staying at Windyhaugh until she organised somewhere to live in her home town of Kelso.

Nana did not take kindly to another woman in her kitchen, especially one as domineering as Janet so the two of them bickered constantly, competing over who could make the best pastry and gingerbread.

Janet was very critical of Nana's housekeeping, in fact, she was in danger of taking over the running of the place, so Nana was always on the lookout for her to make a false move. Her opportunity came one morning, when Janet was emptying her chamber pot down the drain outside. Of all things, a trip bus full of people went past, (It must have been lost!) Nana rounded on Janet triumphantly.

"Janet! Fancy emptying yon thing in front of all thor folk!" Janet however was quite unabashed, and dismissed Nana 's objection with a,"Hout! If they've never used yin, they'll no ken what it's for!" and continued bustling about organising things to her liking.

I quite liked great Aunt Janet.

Her return journey from Australia had brought her through the South Pacific, where she had apparently blessed several tropical islands with a visit. She had a fascinating collection of beautiful shells and artefacts from these exotic places, which she would show me and let me play with, if I was careful.

Aunt Janet was also a fine needlewoman, and though I hadn't the skill or patience to do it myself. I very much admired her beautiful embroidery. My sister and I still have some examples of her work, which she kindly gave us, and my niece, Stephanie, seems to have inherited her great aunt's skill with the needle.

The other thing about Janet I remember is her toast. Whenever she raised a glass she would say,
"Here's tae us! Wee's like us? Gay few, and they're all dead!"

Later that year$_1$ after my return to Tyneside, Bill had taken Nana and Granda out for the day in his newly acquired car. Jim was away, so that left Janet in sole charge of the household.

"If wee're no back by the darkenin', bide in the hoos, shut the door and dinna open it for neebody exceptin' us." Granda advised.

Dusk fell, and having milked the cow and shut in the ducks and hens, Janet locked the door and retired to the fireside with her needlework.

Soon afterwards, Tom Brodie from Blindburn, not realising that Granda was away, called at the house for a chat with Granda on the merits of his sheep, soon bound for Kelso tup sale.

He was surprised to find the house locked, but seeing a light within, he knocked on the door. According to Tom, Janet ignored the knocking for a while, then, affecting a quavering voice, she called out anxiously, There's naebody in but me, — and aah'm daft!"

Tom retraced his steps to Blindburn, chuckling all the way.

Janet was, of course, far from daft. A very capable and strong-minded lady, she descended like a plague of locusts on the homes of several relatives, before retiring gracefully to Kelso.

Chapter Twenty-one - Bett and Bill.

I think it was that summer that I became aware that uncle Bill was courting. The object of his affection was Bett Brodie, elder of Tom and Jessie of Blindburn's two lovely daughters. Bett was then and is now, a bonny lass, with lovely skin, and a ready wit like her father.

She and Bill made a lively pair, and Bill's car was often seen hurtling up and down the valley with Bett laughing happily in the passenger seat.

Bill and Bet on their Wedding Day

They attended many a "do" at Windyhaugh dance hall, watched over by Bett's father, Tom, puffing thoughtfully on his pipe.

On one such occasion, one of the valleys less popular residents complained loudly,

"Bye Brodie, yer settin' up a hell of a stife Wi' that pipe."

"Aye well" drawled Tom, "I'm a lot nearer to the end of the pipe than you are, and it's doing me no harm."

Tom was a remarkable man. Warm, scholarly and witty, he was the valley's philosopher, and a past master of the put down.
The Ministry Of Defence owned vast tracts of the Cheviot Hills then (and still does.) so the occasional army vehicle passing by was not unusual. Tom was seeing to his sheep in the pens near Blindburn one day, when a land rover containing two army officers pulled up. "Come here my man." Commanded one of them, in the supercilious tones of one who considers himself to be addressing an inferior. Tom, taking his time, ambled over, and leaning on his stick, surveyed these two specimens.

"Are there any women in this valley?" He was asked in tones dripping with condescension. Tom appeared to give the question serious consideration, then answered,
"Aye, we keep yin or two aboot the place, for wor awn use." and with that, returned to his work.

What those two officers and very few others knew until after Tom's death, was that the man they were addressing had been offered a place at Oxford University. He had chosen instead. the life of a hill shepherd, a truly remarkable gentleman, Tom Brodie.

The courtship of Bett and Bill continued throughout the summer and into the winter. One dark evening, Bill's little car was seen by the local" polis", parked in a lonely spot between Windyhaugh and Blindburn. The bobby shone his torch on the solitary black car, so Bill wound his window down and stuck out his dark head inquiringly
.
"Have you had an accident?" asked the concerned bobby
"Not yet!" Replied Bill cheerfully, and wound up his window.

Bett and Bill were married the following year, and for a time, occupied Rowhope, another of the valley homesteads, before settling in another part of the county.

The marriage of Bett and Bill, like most good marriages, had its stormy moments, as two strong characters adjusted to the give and take of partnership.

Whilst tenants at Rowhope, when their son and daughter were still babies, Bill got into the habit of taking off to the Alwinton pub each Saturday night, leaving Bett in lonely isolation to care for the children. One Saturday, as Bill was getting washed and changed for his weekly jaunt, he noticed that Bett too seemed to be getting ready for an outing - wearing her best dress, hair freshly done, and lipstick on. Disconcerted, Bill asked, "Where are you going?"

"I'm going the same place you are, the pub at Alwinton." replied Bett "But what aboot the bairns?" Bill demanded to know, quite outraged. "Aye well, they're your bairns an all, If you can leave them every Saturday night, so can I." Replied Bett firmly.

Needless to say, they both stayed in that Saturday, and after that, a baby sitter was arranged, so that they could go out together occasionally. I think Bett must have inherited something of the wisdom of Solomon, so often displayed by her father.

In later years Bett and Bill moved to a farm in the Tyne valley, where two incidents showed uncle Bill's wicked sense of humour.

The first involved an encounter with a family from somewhere on the outskirts of Newcastle. They, out for a Sunday drive, were picnicking in Bill's hayfield and had it well flattened, which rendered it useless for the cutting planned for next day. Not only did the family refuse to move, they, particularly the father and sons were extremely abusive about it

"It's only bloody grass" being one of their more quotable remarks.

Recognising the impossibility of evicting Mr. and Mrs Lout and their entire brood without some unpleasantness (in any case, the damage had already been done) Bill left them to it.

Next Sunday, when the family awoke and drew their curtains, it was to find Bill, complete with collie dog and shepherds crook picnicking on their front lawn.

Lout senior flung open his window and in impressively colourful language, demanded to know what Bill was doing in his garden. "Oh I'm just having a picnic" replied Bill airily.
"But that's my lawn" bellowed the indignant, indeed almost incoherent Mr. Lout. Bill looked around him with interest, "Is it?" he asked innocently, "I thought it was just grass".

Suspecting that this family story might be a rural version of the urban myth, I asked uncle Bill how he had known which garden to picnic in.
"Oh it was easy" he laughed, "Their van had his name on, I just looked him up in the phone book.

Bett and Bill continued to live and work in the Tyne valley for many years. As he grew nearer to retirement Bill still tended a flock of about 800 sheep, no pushover, even for a younger man. One day he was visited by his boss, who seemed "In high good fettle" and informed Bill with great satisfaction that he had succeeded in buying the adjoining farm along with it's flock, which would now be added to Bill's responsibilities.

"Oh aye?" was the rejoinder "You'll be taking on a lad to help then?"
"Well, no Bill, no. I thought you could manage yourself. I have every confidence in you" the boss replied.
"Right then, that's fine "said Bill. "There's just one thing I'd like to ask, can I have next Monday off?"

Taken aback at this, the boss nevertheless agreed to Bill's request. "But tell me Bill, why do you need next Monday off?" he asked. "Well" smiled Bill, "I'll need the day off to gan down to Parson's to get a rocket fitted up me arse."

Needless to say extra help was forthcoming.

JUST GRASS.

The sun was shining brightly
As Bill whistled on his way
With dog at heel and stick in hand
To check his field of hay.

He mused about the chances
Of getting the hay cut,
Then stopped mid stride, gate open wide !
He knew he'd left it shut.

Parked in his hay field blatantly,
A white and rusting van
Disgorging from its innards
A woman and a man.

Accompanied by their family
One dog, three boys, two girls,
Unpacked their picnic hamper
And a table cloth unfurled.

"And what d'you think you're doing here?"
Bill asked in friendly tone
"We're going to have our dinner
And some fun and then go home."

"Well this here is my hay field,
It's grown to feed the sheep
You and your van are spoiling it,
It's enough to make me weep !"

"Don't be such a kill joy,
We're just out for the day,
We aren't doing any harm
Here in your field of hay."

"We can see it's only grass,
When all is said and done
Some bumpkin with a dog and stick
Will not spoil our fun !"

"Fair enough" said William
Continuing on his way
"It's a pity you're so ignorant
As can't tell grass from hay."

The following Sunday morning
In a suburb of the town,
The family drew their curtains,
Disbelievingly looked down.

On their front lawn sat William
With picnic spread around
"Your name was on the van" said he,
"I knew where you'd be found."

"What do you think you're doing?"
The angry fellow yelled,
"This is private property
And that's my lawn as well."

Bill looked around with interest
At where his meal was spread,
"That's strange, I thought it was just grass,"
With twinkling eyes he said.

Jet Propelled.

A jaunty figure William cut
As he strode home through the sheep
The day's work over, supper beckoned
Then a good nights sleep

But standing in his doorway
The owner of the land
Smiled at Bill and clapped his back
And shook him by the hand

"Congratulate me William
I've bought the farm next door
So we'll have near twice the flock
That we have had before"

"Oh Aye" says Bill with caution
"Who is this 'we' you quote
Are you coming to help me
Or hire another bloke?"

"Dear me Bill not at all man
I'm quite sure you can cope
You have my complete confidence"
And other such soft soap

"That's fine" said Bill, "I'll manage
But just one thing I ask
I'll need to take next Monday off
To carry out a task"

"By all means do so William"
The puzzled farmer sighed
"What will you be doing
Taking Bett out for a ride?"

"Oh no" said Bill, "This extra work
Could turn into a farce
So on Monday I'll ask Parsons
For a rocket up my arse!"

Chapter Twenty-Two - Rowhope with Peg.

I would be about nine or ten when I spent my usual summer up the valley at Rowhope instead of Windyhaugh. At that time, it was the home of Aunty Peg, her husband, and family of four sons and one baby daughter. (The family was later increased by a further two girls.)

Nana and Granda had by that time left Windyhaugh, which had been taken over by a Scottish family with a pretty dark haired daughter, named Mary. Uncle Jim stayed on at Windyhaugh to work for them, and in fact, later married Mary.

Rowhope soon became a great favourite with me. Even more isolated than Windyhaugh, it was set in a spur off the main valley in a fork of the Rowhope burn.

The house and farm buildings were set in a straight line facing one branch of the burn, while the other branch gurgled away beyond the stackyard and hayshed at the back. Rowhope's internal arrangements were linear too.

Inside the door was the scullery and walk in pantry. Leading from there was the kitchen/living room, next was the sitting room which was rarely used and whose main purpose in Peg's day was to house her collection of beautiful fuscia plants. Through from there was the staircase, and a bathroom - luxury indeed, with hot and cold running water (when the fire was on) and a flush toilet. It was strange to have a bath in such splendour. I thought back to the days of the tin bath at Windyhaugh.

In those days, when all resources were carefully husbanded, people even mended their saucepans, hawkers were eagerly greeted if they could provide the circular metal pan menders which could eke out the life of a treasured pan a while longer. Nana went one further. When the tin bath sprang a leak, she got Granda to fix it with one of her hawker-bought pan menders. It did the trick too, but she should have warned us of its presence. Poor Alan nearly did himself a serious mischief one evening. He was luxuriating in the tin bath in front of the fire, but Alan could never just sit in the bath, no he had to skid up and down it. He skidded up the bath all right, but the skid back down never happened. Alan leaped to his feet clutching his rear end and screaming, "Ow! Me bum! " The pan mender lurking in the bottom of the bath had caught on Alan's bottom as it skidded past!

Apart from its function of singing me to sleep at night, and providing endless amusement during the day, the burn also served a more practical purpose. It was ideal for washing nappies. Aunty Peg battered them unmercifully against a rock at the edge of the burn, then anchored them there in the running water until they were gleaming white.

The baby, Betty, was a brown eyed, rosy-cheeked little mite. I loved to push her in her pram up and down the bumpy track, which led from Rowhope and its neighbour, The Trows, down to the main part of the valley.

Aunty Peg always warned me not to lift her out until I got back, but she was such an appealing little thing, that on one occasion, I couldn't resist picking her up for a cuddle.

I was to regret it almost immediately. With a gleeful shriek, she grabbed my long plaits and hung on like a leech. I was unable to prize her podgy little fists from my hair, and so had to struggle all the way back pushing the pram with one hand, and bearing her considerable weight with the other. There wasn't much fear of her falling though, she had a grip on my hair like a Scotsman on a five-pound note! Betty and I are still very attached to each other, but in kinship and friendship only.

Summers at Rowhope were to be as happy and carefree as those at Windyhaugh. I had plenty of playmates, as my sister, Linda, was old enough to accompany me sometimes, and Alan's younger brothers were as keen as he was to build dams along the burn. Many a happy hour was spent splashing about in the numerous small pools and waterfalls, to the annoyance of the pied wagtails who bounced about by the burn.

The burn was a source of relaxation in the evenings too. As soon as it got dark, Aunty Peg, the two older boys and I would don our coats and wellies and go out armed with a tin of worms, a torch and a hazel stick, from which dangled a piece of string and a bent pin. We crept along the banks of the burn, keeping a weather eye open for the water bailiff. Peg would shine the torch into a likely pool and Alan, David or I would lower the bent pin with its skewered worm down into the water. We were usually lucky and came home triumphantly bearing a fat brown trout or two.

Sometimes, we gave the fishing a miss and walked the few miles to Barrow burn for what our neighbours over the border would call a ceilidh.

On one such evening, Aunty Peg, having fed and watered the family, called out "Howay bonny lass, we'll away te Barrowburn for a bit crack."

I beamed in anticipation - I loved walking in the valley, and loved even more having Aunty Peg to myself. We set off along past the front of the house and buildings. The dogs barked as we passed their door, but Peg silenced them with a "Hout! Shut up yee dergs."

We had rounded the corner of the byre and passed the door behind which the ducks were locked for the night, when Aunty Peg stopped dead in her tracks. There, no more than five yards in front of us, sitting on the gatepost, was what I took at first to be an owl.

"A hawk'." Breathed Peg. Then in outraged tones, "Thor bugger's eftor ma ducks'."

Indeed the hawk did seem to be staring at the door behind which the ducks were incarcerated.

"Right! Aah'll fettle the flamer,' bide here" declared Peg, striding back round the corner.

She re-emerged seconds later, wielding the large mucking out shovel from the byre.

Without breaking her stride, or in any way trying to disguise her intention, Peg walked straight up to the transfixed hawk, lifted the shovel, and whacked the unfortunate bird on the head, flattening it with one blow.

Propping the shovel against the gatepost recently vacated so dramatically by the deceased hawk, Peg rubbed her hands together with satisfaction and set off down the road to Barrowburn.

The Unfortunate Hawk

"Howay then bonny lass. We'll hetta get crackin' if we're gannin' to Barrowburn the night."

No further mention was made of the demise of the hawk, but I noticed Peg surveying her ducks with a particularly fond smile next day.

You may wonder how housewives did their shopping in those days up the valley. Private cars were as rare as hen's teeth, and in any case, were much too special to be used for hauling groceries.

Watson the carrier filled that role. Once a week his battered old lorry with a tarpaulin top, looking, like a motorised covered wagon, clanked up the winding valley road, bringing sugar, flour and other staples to the isolated homes. He also carried a small stock of sweeties. Not a particularly exciting selection compared to sweetie shops in town, but for a little girl standing on tip toe to peer into the back of the lorry in that lonely valley, there was never so appetising an array as this.

I always accompanied Aunty Peg to the Rowhope road end for her rendezvous with the carrier, and she never failed to spend a little of her housekeeping money on some sweeties for the children.

The walk to meet the carrier was a regular weekly event, a walk to Barrowburn or The Trows was an occasional pleasure, but there was one particular walk which Peg took only once while I was there. It was in the company of a very amorous cow, to Blindburn, home of the Brodies.

Peg's normally placid house cow had become extremely restless and very vocal, so she threw a rope round its neck and set off for the nearest bull. The cow seemed to know where it was going, and why, and took off enthusiastically on the most direct route to Blindburn's handsome bull. Straight through the burn and over the hill she went with indecent haste, Peg hanging valiantly onto the rope, feet flailing.

I had been running about the hill barefoot, as Pegs children sometimes did in the summer. It was one of the perks of staying with Aunty Peg, I loved the feel of the soft grass underfoot and the springy heather pushing up between my toes.

Suddenly I heard Peg's voice yelling at the impatient cow, "Howld on, ye sex mad aad besom Slow doon, or aah'l tek ye back and lock ye in the byre."

As far as I could tell, Peg hadn't a hope of carrying out her threat. The amorous cow was hell bent on reaching the Blindburn bull immediately, if not sooner. She was trailing Peg along in her wake like a speedboat with a water skier.

Always on the look out for a distraction, I ran to catch up.
"Where's the cow takin' ye Aunty Peg?"
A perfectly innocent inquiry, I thought. The effect on Peg however, was electrifying. She screeched to a halt, yanking on the rope with such force, that the poor cow was pop eyed.
"TAKIN' ME?" She bellowed indignantly, "TAKIN" ME INDEED"
"Can ye no see aah'm takin' hor te Tom Brodie's bull."
With that, she regained control of the situation, shortening the rope so that she had the cow's head almost under her arm. Having reasserted her authority, she and the cow set off up the hill again at a more dignified gait. I walked with them almost to the hilltop, but the entertainment seemed to be over, so I lost interest and headed back to Rowhope to play in the burn.

It occurred to me later that it might have been worth staying the course, at least to the top of the hill. I'll bet Aunty Peg had the devil's own job controlling that cow on the downhill run to Blindburn!

A feature of life with Aunty Peg was her singing. It was abominable! Seldom have I heard a more tuneless, toneless sound issuing from the throat of a human being, but Peg didn't care. She raised her voice in song whenever the spirit moved her, and those of us in the vicinity just had to suffer. Peg sang in the house, in the byre, on the hill - anywhere, with gay abandon and commendable volume.
If anyone complained, she just said, "The Lord gave me this voice, so He can bloody well listen te it!"

I'll bet the Lord is a lot more careful about dishing out voices after an earful of Peg's offerings,

One morning, I came downstairs to find Aunty Peg drifting around the kitchen, a distant light in her eye and a smile on her face

"What's the matter Aunty Peg, are ye all right?" I asked anxiously. "Ehhh, I had a lovely dream last night" she answered, frying pan akimbo and a look of absolute bliss on her face. "I dreamed I was an opera singer at Covent Garden, and I brought the house down."

I'm ashamed to say, I roared with laughter. The only way Aunty Peg's voice would bring a house down would be by sheer volume!

The cow she would a bulling go.

The cow was getting noisier
As every hour went by
She threw her head back mooing
To the Dales and hills and sky

Said aunty Peg, "I'll have to
Take the cow to Blindburn's bull
You bairnies can come with me
But diven't act the fool"

The cow, so quite usually
Was deafening to hear
Peg set off up the hill with her
We followed in the rear

Our bare feet in the summer grass
We scampered in the sun
My cousins and myself, our days
Were full of endless fun

The cow plodded on noisily
As Peg heaved on her tether
A funny group we must have looked
As we climbed the hill together

Peg puffed and heaved and sweated
The cow yelled loud and long
Even the summer skylarks
Were halted in their song

At last we reached the hilltop
And Blindburn lay in sight
The cow, transformed, set off at speed
And ran with all her might

Downhill she fairly hurtled
But Peg held on the rope
Her legs, they worked like pistons
I didn't think she'd cope

"Hold on ye silly beastie"
I heard poor Peggy yell (well, it began with 'b' anyway)
But the desperate cow could see the bull
And hear him now as well

We poured on down the hillside
The cow with Peg in tow
But judging from the things she said
She didn't want to go (not at that speed anyway)

Peg reached Blindburn before us
(Assisted by the cow)
The farmer's wife, kind Jessie
Called "come in here bairns, now"

She gave us cups of tea and cake
We were right royally fed
"Where's our cow," young David said
"She's gone off to be wed!"

I didn't quite believe her
But enjoying cake and pie
I wasn't going to tell Jess
That I thought she'd told a lie

The homeward walk to Rowhope
Was quiet and sedate
The cow was left at Blindburn
To contemplate her fate

We brought her back the next week
She sauntered home in style
And I'm sure to this day
On her face she wore a smile.

Chapter Twenty-Three - Blind Billy.

As well as the house cows, the poultry, the cats and sheep dogs, there were usually one or two pet lambs about the farm. One of the pet lambs at Rowhope had a special place in everyone's heart. His name was Billy, and he was blind. This would seem on the face of it to be a terrible handicap for an animal, but not a bit of it. Billy would come to the paddock fence when called, and seemed to know by some sixth sense how to avoid blundering into it. The other pet lambs were amazingly solicitous and helpful to him. Even when they were very small, they would allow him to rest his chin on their backs, and lead him round like little woolly guide dogs.

One evening, I went out, as usual, carrying the big, black teated bottles to feed the pet lambs, only to find that two of them were missing. One of them was Billy.
"Aunty Peg." I shouted, running back into the house. "Billy and Mary aren't in the paddock". Peg dropped what she was doing and hurried outside to check for herself.
"They might not be ower far off hinny. We'll shout on them, and if they hear us, they'll come."

Linda and the boys joined us, and we searched the environs of the farm, calling for Billy with less and less hope as darkness began to fall.
"Aye well, that's it then bairns. The poor little sowl's likely blundered into the burn. Feed these other lambs then hadaway in. Aah'll hev a bit walk doon te the road end, and see if he's there,"

Aunty Peg collected a torch, then set off down the road. I fell into step beside her with a heavy heart. We scanned the hills on either side, anxiously calling Billy's name as we went. It seemed a futile journey. We were almost at the road end, when we heard the answering bleats.

"There they are, ower yonder!" Shouted Aunty Peg. Through the gloom, we could see two pale shapes making their way down the hill. Billy was in the rear, his chin resting on the rump of his friend, who led him carefully towards us.

"Ye knaw, folks think sheep are stupid, but they canna be that daft." said Aunty Peg softly.

Billy was welcomed back to Rowhope like the prodigal son, as was Mary, his guide. Mind you, we were never very sure whether or not his guide had led him away in the first place!

One of the joys of that summer at Rowhope was a little character of a calf. She was a perfect replica of her dad, who was an Aberdeen Angus, so we called her Ginny-Anngoose. Linda and I vied for the job of taking Ginny-Anngoose her bucket of milk.

Linda and Ginny-Anngoose

Goodness knows why, because she was a perfect little devil! As soon as she saw us approaching her paddock with the bucket, a wicked twinkle would appear in her eye, and she would frisk about like a lamb, bucking, kicking and twirling around. A frisking lamb is one thing, but a burly calf hurling herself about with gay abandon is quite another'. The first time that Linda came into the house and announced that Ginny-Anngoose had kicked the bucket, there was a mass exodus as everyone rushed round the back, expecting to see a corpse. What we found was a naughty calf, looking rather sheepish (if such a thing is possible!) with her bucket of milk spilled all over the paddock.

One of our evening occupations (When we weren't out fishing), was listening to the wireless, and Aunty Peg's well-developed sense of humour meant that comedy programmes were great favourites. Peals of laughter often rang out from the cosy living room as we all listened to Ted Ray, Arthur Askey, Jimmy Edwards and the like.

In common with most people, jokes once heard and appreciated, are then usually consigned to my memory's rubbish bin, but every now and then for no good reason, one sticks in the mind. So it was with one particular joke I heard on Peg's ornate old wireless one evening. I filed it in my brain until the following afternoon, when Aunty Peg, my sister and I walked to Barrowburn to chat with Liza over a cup of tea.

As usual, Mrs. Barton sat by the fireside in her straight-backed chair. Linda and I tucked ourselves onto the window seat and settled down to be "seen and not heard", this was no hardship, as we loved to listen to the beautiful Northumbrian dialect, while Peg, Liza, her daughter, Mary and Mrs. Barton mused over the goings on up the valley. Mrs. Barton rose regally from her chair and lifted down a tin of biscuits from the top shelf of a cupboard.

She offered them to Linda and I as though they were the crown jewels so we deliberated carefully before making our choice. Mrs. Barton returned to her seat and rejoined the conversation, and we munched happily on our biscuits. The talk ranged far and wide before settling on the recent demise of one Duncan from further down the valley.

Old Tom came into the kitchen at this point, parked his stick and lowered himself carefully into a chair. Tom, it seemed had attended Duncan's funeral service. (Funerals in those days were a male preserve, women were not expected to attend.)

"Aye, he had a canny send off, right enough. There was a good turn oot, considerin' it was such a caad day." Apparently the day designated for Duncan's funeral had been the wettest, windiest summer day for years.

"Aah wish aah hadda worn me lang Johns" said Tom. "Aah was bloody freezin', even in the chorch. Everybody else was shiverin' an all. In fact, the warmest one there was Duncan!" he finished, with a wry smile.

Aunty Peg spluttered over her tea, and soon everyone was laughing.

Encouraged by the atmosphere of bonhomie. I spoke up.

"I know a joke. It's about this little boy whose mam was expecting a baby, but he wasn't supposed to know. Well on the Sunday, his dad said, " come and get yer dinner, yer mam's carving" Next day, the dad thought he'd better tell the boy that his mam was expecting, but when he told him, the boy said, "I know", "How do you know?" asked the dad. "You told me yesterday" said the boy, "You said mam was calving".

I gabbled my remembered joke from last night's radio show, and everyone laughed, especially Aunty Peg, even though it was the second time she'd heard it.

Mrs. Barton however, was not amused. Stone faced, she rose to her feet, and pointedly picking up the biscuit tin, she replaced it on the shelf.

I was very quiet on the walk home, pondering on the unpredictability of people's reactions.

I worried for some time that I had offended old Mrs.Barton. However, on my next visit to Barrowburn, she lifted down the biscuit tin again and offered me one, so I must have been forgiven. Perhaps it is just as well that Mrs. Barton is not around to hear some of the jokes bandied about on today's radio and television!

Chapter Twenty-Four - Rowhope With Bett And Bill.

A couple of summers later, Aunty Peg moved to another farm. but, to my delight, uncle Bill and Aunty Bett moved into Rowhope, and uncle Jim and Aunty Mary took up residence in the neighbouring farm, The Trows.

Linda and I arrived for our summer visit looking forward to "helping" Aunty Bett with daughter, Carol, a blonde little thing, and the double of her granddad, Tom Brodie.

Idyllic days passed, messing about in the water, teaching yet another batch of hen reared ducklings to swim and making wild flower gardens on the banks of the burn. That these were immediately platched over by ducks and trampled by cows, did not deter us in the least. We simply re planted our garden the next day.

Something in the walled garden next to the house must have held a powerful attraction for butterflies, because there were always dozens of them in or around the house. We invariably shared our bedroom with three or four of them, resting just inside the sash window.

Mum and dad came to stay for a few days once, and they ended up sharing their room with something larger than a butterfly. We became aware of the intruder at about five o clock one morning, when mam's shrieks could be heard reverberating round the house.

"There's a vulture on top of the wardrobe!" she screamed, as she hurtled out of the bedroom door. Never having seen a vulture in the flesh before, I crept round the door to have a look. On top of the wardrobe sat ———a pigeon! Admittedly, it did have its back hunched in a vulture like attitude, but it was most definitely a pigeon.

The bedroom window was open, so it had probably flown in the previous evening and roosted there, unnoticed, until mam opened her eyes and saw it looming over her in the early morning light.

Aunty Bett, Linda and I would sometimes walk Carol in her pram just up the road to The Trows, to visit Aunty Mary. The only problem with this. was the large flock of geese, which also lived at The Trows.

The first part of our walk would be a pleasant meander - the track followed the path of the burn, which gurgled a counter point to Carol's baby cooing. Once we got to The Trows farm gate however, the walk took on an entirely different character. We would scan the landscape anxiously like marauding mercenaries, looking for signs of lurking geese. If the coast was clear, we would creep quietly through the gate, wincing at each give away creak of its rusty hinges, and then run, hell for leather for the house. Invariably, we would get half way there, when the geese would appear round the corner of one of the farm buildings swooping towards us like valkyries, necks and wings outstretched and hissing nastily. We would close ranks round the pram and shake our sticks at them to keep them at bay until we reached the sanctuary of the house.

Carol seemed to enjoy this last part of our expedition best. shrieking with laughter as we bounced her over the rutted track.
I think she thought the geese appeared solely for her amusement. I must confess, they scared me to death. I wasn't surprised to read recently that some factories deploy them instead of guard dogs they have the added advantage that they can be eaten after they have served their turn. I wouldn't fancy roast Alsatian!

One day, I went to the Trows with uncle Bill. The geese were no problem in his company. He strode through them as though they didn't exist and they didn't bother him at all, probably because he had two sheep dogs at his heels who looked as though they wouldn't stand any nonsense. I skipped along beside uncle Bill, feeling quite brave in his shadow and stuck my tongue out at the gander.

We were on our way to see the new bull, a recent arrival at the Trows, which uncle Jim was keen to show off. The dogs lay down in a patch of sunshine, pink tongues lolling, and we joined uncle Jim leaning on the gate and surveyed the enormous beast. He was a Hereford, with the distinctive brown and white markings of his breed, and a large dewlap hanging between his front legs. He swung his huge head in our direction, dewlap wobbling, and gave us a disinterested stare, before lowering his be-ringed nose back to the grass he had been chewing with infinite concentration.

I observed him closely. He didn't look at all dangerous, standing there peacefully in the sunshine, and it was hard to imagine anything so huge travelling at speed. I was wearing red, and he hadn't even given me a second look, rather disappointing considering all the hair raising stories I'd heard about mad bulls. I lost interest in him and hitched from one foot to the other, waiting for uncle Bill to escort me back through the geese, so that I could return to Rowhope.

Conversation round the table that evening turned to the bull and the quality of calves he would produce.

Linda listened in silence for a while, then a puzzled expression settled on her face.
"What I want to know is, how do you tell the difference between a cow and a bull?"
Uncle Bill's mouth opened, then snapped shut again. While he and Aunty Bett looked at each other, I spoke up.
"That's easy, stupid. The bull has his milk bag at the front."
Uncle Bill hastily left the table and went into the scullery, from whence the sound of strangulated laughter could be heard. Linda seemed quite happy with my answer to her question, so the matter was settled.

Evenings with Bett and Bill were similar to those spent at Windyhaugh. Uncle Bill taught us various card games, amidst much hilarity and cheating, while Thomas, their very superior black and white cat sat upright in the hearth, staring down his nose at such goings on. There was a wind up gramophone too, and of course, uncle Bill's yarns.

Before moving to Rowhope, they had lived for a time on a farm on the Scottish side of the border. This was a large establishment, and the work force was housed in two rows of stone cottages.

In one cottage lived Lizzie and her brother, Tom, Who must have looked like Jack Spratt and his wife, of nursery rhyme fame. Tom was small and slight, but his sister, Lizzie, who kept house for him, was an enormous, rather well covered lady.

One day, whilst shopping in the little town, she stepped onto some scales, to discover that she weighed eighteen stone. Lizzie was shocked. "Bugger me!" she exclaimed, "Another twa pund an' I'll be a ton!" No one disabused her of this notion, and it didn't stop her from consuming food in vast quantities.

The baker's van used to call every week. and it was Lizzie's habit to purchase three hot pies for lunch that day - two for her and one for Tom! One day, the three steaming hot pies were put on the windowsill to cool and a farm cat, seizing his opportunity, made off with one of them.

When Tom came home from his morning's work, he was greeted by Lizzie, wringing her hands and saying,
"Eeh Tom, the cat's got yer pie!"

Needless to say Lizzie consumed her two!

One shopkeeper in the nearby town must have been rather exasperated with Lizzie, when she entered their genteel establishment one December.

She was after a pair of gloves as a Christmas present for uncle Bill,

"What size hands has he got madam?" inquired the plummy voiced assistant.

"I dinna ken" said Lizzie. Then added helpfully. 'But he has a hell of a big foot!"

Chapter Twenty-Five - Jen's Wedding.

I was aware that summer that the valley was buzzing with barely suppressed excitement. Female relatives of Aunty Bett that I'd never met before, kept turning up at Rowhope to chatter animatedly about dresses and flowers, and the merits of various hats, bags, and shoes.

One of these visitors was a girl so breathtakingly beautiful, that I was quite overawed. A cousin of Bett's from further down the valley, she was tall and slim with corn coloured blonde hair, sky blue eyes and the beautiful complexion common to many of Bett's family. I didn't think such creatures existed outside the screen of our cinema at home.

It was the first time in my life that I had beheld such beauty in the flesh, and I was fascinated. It was whilst loitering about, mesmerised by this stunning creature, that I finally overheard the reason for all the excitement, Jen was getting married.

Jen was Aunty Bett's younger sister. She was actually christened Jeanette, but I never heard her called by that name. She worked as a shepherdess for her father at Blindburn and was to marry Howard, a shepherd from the adjoining farm, so naturally, the whole valley was astir with preparations for the great day.

The time of the wedding was drawing near, and Aunty Bett still hasn't found an outfit for the occasion.. so when an intrepid Indian peddler (complete with turban) hauled his suitcase of goods all the way to Rowhope on foot, he was greeted with open arms. The suitcase was flung open on the living room floor and Aunty Bett delved into its contents with enthusiasm.

The room was soon strewn with garments of every hue, while Bett flitted from one outfit to the other, alighting on one for a while, then swooping on another, like a butterfly fluttering between flowers. Eventually, she made her choice, a beautiful glazed floral cotton dress with matching jacket. She looked lovely in it as she twirled around to show it off to a bemused Uncle Bill and a beaming Indian peddler. It is a tribute to the man's enthusiasm and determination that he was prepared, with no means of transport, to hawk his goods to our isolated outpost on the off chance of making a sale, so I am glad he happened on a time when everyone in the valley was looking for something new to wear. He made sales in most of the valley's homesteads, and deservedly so.

As well as her wedding outfit, Aunty Bett had been much taken with a fine wool sweater with bat-wing sleeves in the very latest style. After some deliberation, she added this to her list of purchases, much to the disgust of uncle Bill. Latest style or not, he wasn't impressed by it. The sweater was dismissed with.
"No, I care nowt for that. It hides all yer curves."

As the day of the wedding drew nearer, it dawned on me that Linda and I would still be at Rowhope, and were to be included in the celebrations. My excitement was muted by discomfort, when I realised that we had nothing to wear for the occasion. When mam had packed our suitcase back in Newcastle, she had chosen clothes suitable for our usual valley holiday. We'd had in mind plodging in the burn, running about the hills and playing with animals, certainly not an important event like a wedding.

We could hardly repay Jen's kindness in inviting us by showing up at her wedding in faded old frocks and battered sandals. With heavy heart, I confided in Aunty Bett the shortcomings of our wardrobe and suggested that we stay at home to look after the animals.

"Nowt the kind!" she dismissed my worries airily. "I'll sharp kit the two of ye oot, nae bother."

Her wardrobe door was flung open and clothes were lifted out, weighed up and discarded, until she found something which met with her approval.

A pretty print dress with puffed sleeve", was decided upon to be taken in and up to fit Linda, but I could hardly believe my good fortune at the beautiful outfit chosen for me. It must have been a souvenir from Bett's recent girl-hood, when she was a frequent attender of dances in Alnwick and Rothbury.

I had never worn anything so beautiful or so grown up. It was an emerald green satin top and circular skirt, but what made it so special was the black overskirt which had a pattern of tiny holes all over it, allowing the satin beneath to shimmer through like emerald green stars in a black sky.

To wear something so glamorous was beyond my wildest dreams. In the years since then, I have worn several dresses which have been elegant or pretty as the occasion demanded, but never have I felt so thrilled to wear anything as I was with Aunty Bett's black and green skirt. I could hardly wait for the wedding day to arrive.

On the great day we were an exited party, as we climbed carefully into uncle Bill's car. He was very handsome in his suit and Aunty Bett even prettier than usual in her chosen outfit. Carol was a little picture in a lemon organdie frock and Linda and I preened ourselves in our borrowed finery.

Jen was a beautiful bride her chestnut curls dancing in the sunlight, Howard, seeming quite overwhelmed by his good fortune beamed with pride in his vivacious new wife.

It was a happy day, with relatives of all ages, shapes and sizes congratulating the happy couple.

Some of the children raced around between the adults, shouting with laughter. Such behaviour was of course, quite beneath me with my new grown up image. I must have been insufferable, as I wandered about with a regal air, taking every opportunity to make sweeping turns which made the circular skirt swish round me dramatically.

The day was rounded off by a dance. Not in Windyhaugh dance hall, but in a village hall further down the valley, which rather unusually, was on the first floor. The flight of stairs leading up to it was negotiated with exaggerated care by some of the men, as the night wore on and the many toasts to bride and groom began to take effect.

The evening "do" was a boisterous affair, the band played their hearts out and the "caller" of the dances did a good job in persuading most people to take to the floor. For a long time, Linda and I sat on the sidelines beside a couple of collie dogs. Then we realised that not knowing the dances was no drawback.

The caller shouted instructions for each one ,and anyway, enthusiasm rather than skill seemed to be what was called for, so we hurled ourselves into the melee with a will. A weather eye had to be kept open for those men wearing tackety boots.

A kick on the shin from one of those would break your ankle like a stick, but that hazard apart, the dance was great fun.

It was a day I was sorry to see the end of.

Chapter Twenty-Six - Progress?

During successive summers up the valley, I had noticed that change, however slowly, was taking place.

Some were changes made by individual farmers and shepherds. The major changes however, were brought about by the biggest landowner up the valley, The Ministry Of Defence. I have mentioned that visitors to the valley were rare. This was partly due to the fact that private cars were much scarcer then, but more especially due to the fact that the valley was almost a closed community, as the army had it barricaded off for much of the time.

The reason for this was, the surrounding hills were a M.o.D. training area, so if you went wandering around off the road, you were liable to be blown sky high. Hence 'the barrier', a bar, which came down over the road, manned by a soldier in a sentry box.

I can well imagine the M.o.D. not wishing to be responsible for blowing up a stray tourist or two, but gradually, they began to realise that tourists weren't too keen on the idea either, and could be trusted to stick to the road during war games. Eventually therefore, the barrier was done away with, and the road up the valley opened to the public..

Red flags were still flown as a warning to stick to the beaten track, and initially, each farmstead was visited by an army motorcyclist to warn of firing times. This was to avoid the possibility of an incautious shepherd being blasted to smithereens.

Mind you, local rumour had it that there were some unscrupulous farmers who, on receiving these warnings, would hurriedly herd their oldest, most decrepit sheep right into the firing line, in order to collect compensation from the M.o.D.

The army later installed telephones in several strategically placed farms, to cut down on the need for motorcycle messengers. Electricity too came to the valley and lamp lit evenings became a thing of the past, and so progress gradually eroded the old pattern of life.

The valley people themselves instigated some changes. For instance, one summer I was sad to see Granda using a hay baler, the uniform blocks of hay it produced completely lacked the charm of a field full of pikes. Almost as bad, he bought a dreadful machine which looked like a preying mantis to lift the bales onto the top of the pile in the hayshed. This was the elevator, all my resentment at the passing of our previous happy hay making customs was directed at it, and many was the venomous glance I shot at the wretched thing.

These changes in valley life first struck me forcibly when, passing Windyhaugh one year on my way to Rowhope, I noticed a sign at the end of the footbridge proclaiming that ice cream was for sale there. The combination of accessibility and electricity was being cashed in on by the new tenants, and why not I suppose. But that ice cream placard struck a jarring note.
Changes too came to the valley school. The sturdy stone building was closed. A modern one, with an inordinate amount of glass used in its construction (rather foolish, considering northern winters) was built on the flat ground next to the dance hall. However, this too eventually closed, and valley children have to travel to Harbottle, then on to Rothbury and Morpeth to complete their education.

Of course there are fewer children up the valley nowadays. Not only because families tend to be smaller, but also because there are fewer families living there.

Modern technology means that smaller numbers of men can care for larger numbers of sheep. It is quicker getting round them on a quad bike than on foot or even horseback., and of course, electric clippers can shear sheep quicker than the old hand shears. Some hill slopes have been cleared of sheep altogether to make way for the rows of conifers, so beloved of the Forestry Commission. (Nana would have no trouble finding "a bit stick" now.) In fact, Aunty Peg actually helped to plant some of the hillsides above Blindburn, glad of the forestry money to help rear her family.

Some of the farmsteads stand empty now, except for occasional invasions of soldiers, some of them speaking languages never heard up the valley before, when NATO troops engage in exercises there. I wonder what these young men from countries like Belgium and Holland think of this lonely and lovely valley. Do they ever give a passing thought to the previous incumbents of the empty stone houses, like Carshope, and most tragically. Barrowburn? Indeed, what would past residents think if they could see their homes, each one of which was the centre of a little world, standing neat and tidy ——— and empty.

No doubt, life is much easier for those residents left in the valley, and its comparative isolation means that a strong sense of community does still remain, but the pull of the outside world is strong for the young. It is dangled in front of their faces on TV. every day, and it is accessible now. Many of them leave the valley never to return - this has always been the case of course, but there were always plenty to take their place.

Now, those young men who choose the lonely life of the hill shepherd are finding that wives willing to share their isolation are hard to find.

Never mind, hill men have always been a charming and persuasive breed. I am sure that life in the valley will go on, even if it is a little different to the days I remember.

Up the valley! that's what I say.

Sketch Map of Upper Coquetdale

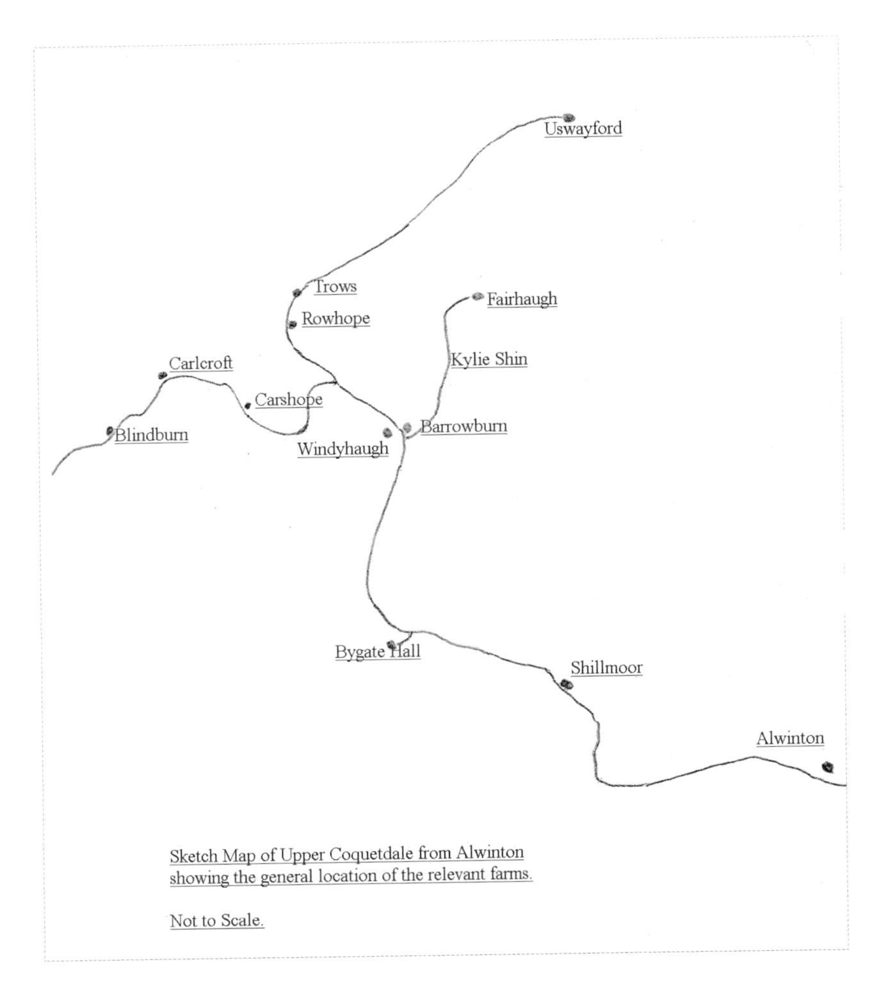

© L.E.Laidler